ENCOUNTERING THE GOD OF LOVE

PORTRAITS FROM THE OLD TESTAMENT

BRAD E. KELLE AND
STEPHANIE SMITH MATTHEWS, EDITORS

THE FOUNDRY
PUBLISHING®

The Foundry Publishing®
PO Box 419527
Kansas City, MO 64141
thefoundrypublishing.com

978-0-8341-3998-5

Printed in the
United States of America

Cover design: Arthur Cherry
Interior design: Sharon Page

Library of Congress Cataloging-in-Publication Data
Names: Kelle, Brad E., 1973- editor. | Matthews, Stephanie Smith, 1988- editor.
Title: Encountering the God of love : portraits from the Old Testament / Brad E. Kelle and Stephanie Smith Matthews, editors.
Description: Kansas City, MO : The Foundry Publishing, 2021. | Includes bibliographical references. | Summary: "The church has a long history of believing that the God of the Old Testament is a different, less loving God than the God of the New Testament. Old Testament scholars have come together to paint a different portrait of our changeless Creator—one that shows God's immutable nature of love and compassion demonstrated in every major section of the Old Testament scriptures"— Provided by publisher.
Identifiers: LCCN 2021003731 (print) | LCCN 2021003732 (ebook) |
ISBN 9780834139985 | ISBN 9780834139992 (ebook)
Subjects: LCSH: God—Love—Biblical teaching. | Bible. Old Testament—Criticism, interpretation, etc.
Classification: LCC BS1192.6 .E53 2021 (print) | LCC BS1192.6 (ebook) | DDC 231—dc23
LC record available at https://lccn.loc.gov/2021003731
LC ebook record available at https://lccn.loc.gov/2021003732

10 9 8 7 6 5 4 3 2 1

CONTENTS

INTRODUCTION

BRAD E. KELLE AND STEPHANIE SMITH MATTHEWS

AS WE PEN THESE WORDS in the midst of a global pandemic, now more than ever we yearn for the God of love. As people of the Book, one way we encounter divine love is through prayerful study of the Scriptures. Yet the Old Testament is rarely the go-to resource today for Christian ministers and laypersons looking for clear proclamations and compelling portrayals of God as one whose nature and actions are love. Sure, the Old Testament has powerful stories of God's mighty acts on behalf of God's people and inspiring psalms in which worshipers declare God's enduring faithfulness. But providing readers with consistent and sustained encounters with a loving God doesn't seem to be the Old Testament's strength—nor its reputation.

There is a long history in the church of discounting the Old Testament when it comes to the proper understanding of God's character, especially in light of the New Testament. For some, that discounting goes further—namely, to a sense that the Old Testament portrayals actually run counter to the nature of God as exemplified in the life of Jesus of Nazareth. In the early centuries of Christianity, a formal teaching associated with the Christian leader Marcion of Sinope in the second century emerged that argued not only that the Old Testament (and much of the New Testament) was irrelevant for Christians but also that the God revealed in the Old Testament was a violent, war-making, lower divine being who was actually an altogether different God from the one revealed in the teachings of Jesus. While the church eventually rejected this belief, its effects have lingered. We see them in the words of both popular speakers and bloggers who directly instruct their followers to unhook the Old Testament from their faith, and also in the more subtle ways that some preachers and laypersons shy away from preaching, teaching, or studying Old Testament passages, considering them unhelpful for proclaiming God's love. Finding clear portrayals of a loving God in the Old Testament remains a challenge. After all, as the common expectations often go, isn't the New Testament just better (or, at least, easier) in this regard?

This book aims to confound those expectations. The idea for this book emerged from near-daily informal conversations about the Old Testament and the church that took place in the hallway between the offices of the book's co-editors. We love the Old Testament (we are Old Testament professors, after all!). We experience the love of God as we prayerfully study the Old Testament. One of the lofty goals of our teaching is to help students become more likely to encounter a loving God as they delve into the Old Testament, and to encourage them to continue that encounter as they worship in local congregations. Even so, we have often discussed with candor and sadness the barriers many Christians have to cultivating an appreciation for the Old Testament. Our conversations turned to the question of how we might provide some resources for preachers, teachers, and laypersons doing the hard work of interpretation, proclamation, teaching, and other ministries, especially with the hope of proclaiming the God of love from the Old Testament.

Out of that desire, this book offers studies of specific passages that expound how each interpreter encounters the God of love in a particular Old Testament text. The overall idea is to show that, in many ways and plenty of places, the Old Testament reveals a loving God. Attention to God's nature as love certainly fits with the Wesleyan theological tradition's insistence that love defines the character of God's saving work in the world and the lifestyle of God's holy people. Each chapter in this book attempts to advance that emphasis by proceeding through selected Old Testament passages to provide a commentary-style Bible study that gives an overall interpretation of the passage with a special focus on how that passage reveals the God of love. The studies are not comprehensive and do not attempt to address every issue that might be relevant for interpreting the passage. The goals are to show how the passage in question functions as a biblical portrait of a loving God, to assist others in using the passage to share that portrait, and to invite readers to reflect on the passage from that perspective. Toward this last goal, each chapter concludes with a series of three discussion questions designed to foster conversation about the passage itself and the portrait of a loving God that can emerge from it.

One of the related goals of this book is to demonstrate that portrayals of God as a God of love are not rare in the Old Testament, nor are they confined only to certain books or sections. Certainly not every passage in the Old Testament portrays God as loving (at least, not on the surface), and some passages in fact seem to create problems for the very notion of a loving God. Nonetheless, the God of love appears at various places and in various ways throughout the whole of the Old Testament. The biblical passages examined here come from every major section of the Old Testament (the Pentateuch, Historical Books, Poetry and Wisdom, and Prophets). We take up specific texts from Genesis, Exodus, Numbers, Deuteronomy, Ruth, 2 Samuel, Ezra, Nehemiah, Psalms, Job, Isaiah, and Hosea. Furthermore, the biblical passages explored include a variety of genres: narratives, poems, rituals, prayers, prophetic oracles, and more. In all these places and in all these forms, today's readers of Scripture can encounter the God of love.

There is another special element to this collection that makes it, in a way, the first of its kind. This book brings together for the first time in a single collection interpretive studies written by those who serve as professors of Old Testament in universities, seminaries, and Bible colleges within the global Church of the Nazarene. It is, of course, not a full representation. Women and men in various parts of Africa, Europe, South America, and other locations of the world teach the Old Testament and contribute academic writings to help both ministers and laypersons. While the contributors to this volume come from several different geographical areas (California, Colorado, Idaho, Tennessee, Kansas, Missouri, Oklahoma, Illinois, Ohio, and the Philippines), it is easy to see the limitations in representation and perspective against the backdrop of a global church. The Old

Testament professors included in this book are nine men and only two women, all from the same racial and ethnic background.

This reality is no indictment of the work contained here; it is simply who we are at the moment in many of our most-established educational institutions in the Church of the Nazarene. Greater diversity among Bible professors would better represent the women and men of our global church. But calling attention to the makeup of this volume is a reminder that all people who read Scripture and encounter the God of love do so from their own contexts and through the lenses of their own experiences. This is good news! The God who became flesh in the person, life, and times of Jesus of Nazareth likewise comes—in the Spirit and through the words of Scripture—to encounter the people of God today in the midst of our personal, communal, and social realities. The contributions offered in this book do not pretend to be objective or final. Rather, they invite engagement of the biblical passages by those who come from different perspectives and may see different things in these portraits of a loving God. The contributors, while limited in perspective and context, attempt to offer some of the fruits of academic biblical studies as a resource to all who may take up these biblical texts as preachers, teachers, and readers and seek a more meaningful engagement with the Old Testament.

Given the nature of this book as a collection of chapters by various authors, a couple of additional caveats may be helpful to the reader. Although we took great care during the editing process, the reader will surely notice some inconsistencies—a few of which, at least, are present by design. We have not, for instance, standardized all biblical quotations to be from a single version. Rather, we have deferred to the individual preferences of the authors and indicated those preferences in the chapters. We also allowed individual authors to arrange the discussion of their chosen biblical passage as they saw fit, even as each chapter revolves around the guiding question of how that particular passage reveals God to be a God of love in the Old Testament. In pursuing that question, some chapters engage a more academic tone or use a more technical approach than others. Hence, some chapters include a number of notes that point the reader to scholarly resources and insights for further study while others proceed in a more informal manner. We have not imposed heavy uniformity but have tried to let each author have her or his say in a way that allows the reader to hear a particular perspective but also invites further reflection and other insights.

In the end, in and through all of the approaches and perspectives offered in this collection, the hope of the work as a whole is to provide a resource for preachers, teachers, and laypersons to see the God of love in the Old Testament. Any careful reader of Scripture likely knows that the Old Testament's portrayals of a loving God are rarely straightforward. As noted already, not every passage in the Old Testament seems to present God as loving, and some passages seem to create problems for that very notion. Simply put, the picture of God in the Old Testament is complicated. Indeed, many books have been written exploring the "problem passages" of the Old Testament. These books can be important and helpful resources. But our task here is to show that the Old Testament testifies to a God whose character and ways are defined by love.

The New Testament may seem simpler—or at least more straightforward. However, if we draw our understanding of God only from the New Testament, we do not get the fullest possible picture of God's nature as revealed in Scripture. There is also something about being willing, with God's help, to deal with the complexity in our Scriptures that can help us do the same in our everyday lives. If we listen attentively to messages from the Old Testament that at first prove difficult to understand, we are preparing ourselves to join God in listening attentively to other people. While the work may be demanding and the results complex, the authors of this volume believe the study of the Old Testament offers readers dynamic and transformative encounters with the God of love.

1. HAGAR, ISHMAEL, AND THE GOD WHO HEARS

GENESIS 21:14–21

STEPHANIE SMITH MATTHEWS

SINCE I WAS A YOUNG GIRL, my life has taken place in conversation with God, including though certainly not limited to prayerful study of the Scriptures. I recall a few of us ten-year-olds informing our Sunday school volunteer, with all our Midwestern politeness, that we were fully capable of rattling off the stories about Moses, Abraham, Jacob, and Joseph, and we were ready for more! Our weekly congregational worship and prayer services had introduced us to a God we could encounter through the abiding presence of the Holy Spirit. Our God was active, challenging, and, above all, with us no matter what we faced in life. I think we yearned for an encounter with that same God in our study of the Scriptures. We didn't just want to hear about God doing miraculous things a very long time ago—we wanted our divine Friend right there with us as we turned the pages of our Bibles together.

In the ensuing years, I began to encounter that God in the midst of youth group studies and sermons on the Gospels and the letters of Paul. They helped me understand the kind of life to which God calls us, and led me into prayers of consecration, asking God to help me live that way through the indwelling of the Holy Spirit. But much of the Old Testament remained a mystery to me. I did read through it in its entirety when I entered my teens. But about the time I hit Leviticus, and extending through the Prophets, I felt as though I were reading above my grade level, theologically speaking.

I was fortunate to be able to continue my study of the Scriptures in college. In the first two days of a class whose intimidating title I still remember (Exilic and Postexilic Prophecy and Community), our professor told us the story of God's people in the Old Testament.[1] He explained the impact of the exile of the Hebrew people from their homeland and suggested that much of what we now call the Old Testament is a conversation between a people and their God as they try to make sense of the communal tragedy they have suffered.

1. That professor, Kevin Mellish, happens to be the author of chapter 6.

Furthermore, the Old Testament gives evidence that there were not always easy explanations for complex situations—but the lines of communication remained open nevertheless.

As a professor of the Old Testament and minister of the gospel, I understand my calling as twofold: (1) removing barriers between people and encountering a God of love in the Old Testament, and (2) walking alongside others in their journeys of faith. There may be any number of barriers people face. Some we mentioned in the introduction. Another significant barrier I encounter in my ministry applies not only to our relationship with the Old Testament but also to the Bible as a whole: dismissal by people in the church of another's deepest cries and concerns. Why should anyone expect to encounter a God of love in the Bible if they do not encounter the love of God from the people of the Book?

A few years ago, when I was going through a difficult time in my life, a wise friend and sister in Christ listened to me and then responded simply, "That sounds hard." She did not try to fix me, nor did she blame me or downplay my struggles. She saw my situation and heard my cry. I cried some cathartic tears that night and have remembered to use those words when others share their struggles with me—because sometimes all it takes to experience love is to have our struggles acknowledged, to be seen and heard. If possible, those who see and hear will participate in the path to healing. As the people of God, our seeing and hearing communicates that the God we serve sees and hears too. Across the pages of the Old Testament, we find a God who accompanies the people—goes with them in their journey of faith. Sometimes God intervenes with miraculous power. Other times God simply comes alongside, sees, and hears.

Hagar's Encounter with God

In what follows, I invite you to enter into a conversation with God through a close reading of Genesis 21:14–19.[2] Its main characters are Hagar; her child, Ishmael; God; and a messenger from God. Abraham, Sarah, and Isaac lurk in the background since, without them, the events of this passage would never have happened.

You may wish to pause and read through the passage in the translation of your choice.[3] Glance at the verses just before and after the passage to get a sense of the surrounding literary context. As you read, consider the experience of each person involved. Then take your time and note what words, phrases, or images stand out to you.

When you are ready, return to this text, where I will discuss some of the phrases and images that struck me in my study of the passage. Afterward, I will consider the symbolic possibilities of these images as we contemplate the passage with each other and with God.

Containers of Water (vv. 14a, 15a, 19)

Abraham rose early in the morning,
took food and ***a container of water*** *and gave them to Hagar;*

When the water from the container was empty . . .

God opened her eyes and she saw:
a well of water!

---

2. This passage details a threat to the life of a child. Those who have experienced such loss may find the passage distressing to read. In small group settings where this is the case, you may wish to move on to chapter 8 of this book, which includes an account of encountering the love of God in the wake of grief.

3. I will offer my own translations but will take some poetic license in order to highlight the dramatic effect I perceived in my reading of the original Hebrew (and, occasionally, of the ancient Greek translation called the Septuagint). For this reason, you may wish to read the passage on your own first, from a more traditional translation.

She went and filled the container with water
and gave the boy a drink.

There is irony in Abraham's provision of a skin of water to Hagar as he simultaneously cut her off from the supply he used to fill it. That container would only last Hagar and Ishmael a limited amount of time as they wandered the wilderness. The end result was inevitable: if Hagar was unable to find another water source, both she and her child would die. This expected outcome sets up the tension of the short narrative. In the end, God led Hagar to another source of water, from which she could refill the container and replenish her son. But Hagar did not know that was to be the outcome.

I wonder about that charged moment as the water skin passed from Abraham to Hagar. Did its inadequacy weigh on both their minds in that moment? Was Abraham too filled with shame to make eye contact with the slave he impregnated and was now sending away, or did he hold her gaze in an attempt to convince everyone, including himself, that his actions were justified because God had not intervened to stop him? Perhaps Hagar lifted her face or positioned their son in such a way as to remind Abraham of what he was doing. Or she may have already written him off, ready to shake off the dust of this place and its abuse and set her eyes on a new type of survival for herself and her son. Whether looking forward with steely resolve, riddled with anxiety, or some combination of both, Hagar set out with one skin of water that would be incapable of sustaining them for the journey to come.

I pause here, thinking about the barriers we can unintentionally erect between God's children and the loving God made manifest in the elements of our faith. Imagine if Abraham, as he handed over the skin of water, said to Hagar, "God loves you." Any truth in those words would be rendered ridiculous, utterly incompatible with the actions of God's chosen covenantal partner. If Hagar did hold out hope in a God of love and provision, such faith would have existed in spite of the example of her slave owners.

A Burden to Bear (vv. 14–15, 18a, 19)

Abraham rose early in the morning,
took food and a container of water and gave them to Hagar;
he put them on her shoulder, along with the child,
and sent her away;
she departed and wandered in the wilderness of Beersheba.

When the water from the container was empty,
she cast the child under one of the bushes.

"Stand up! Pick up the boy and hold him tight with your hand . . ."

God opened her eyes and she saw:
a well of water!
She went and filled the container with water
and gave the boy a drink.

Hagar shouldered the burden of carrying the skin of water as well as the child. Whether she carried her child or he walked alongside her, she bore the burden of knowing the water skin would not provide water for both of them indefinitely. In fact, our passage is framed by her concern and provision for her child. First Abraham "took food and a skin of water and gave them to Hagar; he put them on her shoulder, along with the child, and sent her away" (v. 14). In the next verse, we are told the water was gone, and "she cast the child under one of the bushes" (v. 15). The food and water weighed on her as she carried them, but they weighed on her in a different way once they were gone. As the physical burden of the water skin lightened, the urgency of finding a new water source increased.

Finally the container emptied, along with her hopes. She "cast down" her child and "lifted up" her voice, making known her pain. The burden of watching her child die, she said, was too much to bear: "Do not let me see the death of the child" (v. 16). Hagar's cry, whether screamed, murmured, or made incomprehensible through sobs, speaks for itself. The death of a child is incomprehensible.

At this moment, God sends a messenger who tells her to walk back over to Ishmael and take him fast by the hand. Usually, the image of holding fast to a young child's hand brings to mind for me a rambunctious toddler straining to run off and indulge their sense of wonder at the world. In this case, Ishmael would not have had the energy, near as he was to death. Was Hagar to grasp his hand in comfort, to lend the little strength she had left? With this initial instruction, Hagar may have wondered if God's messenger had appeared to give *her* strength to do what she did not think she could bear, and what none should have to bear.

Indeed, there was no one else there to lament, grieve, and accompany Hagar and Ishmael through the unspeakable. Often we encounter God's love in those messengers from God who accompany us in our grief. Those who sit with us, relieve us of the other burdens of life, and say, "That's hard"—or nothing at all. Sometimes we feel close to God in those moments. Other times we are numb, knowing rather than sensing God's presence with us. In the case of Ishmael and Hagar, God's messenger is able to point her to a source of water that will save both their lives. The water skin that had become useless now becomes the container through which Hagar delivers fresh, lifesaving water to her child.

She Went and Wandered (vv. 14, 16a, 19)

Abraham rose early in the morning,
took food and a container of water and gave them to Hagar;
he put them on her shoulder, along with the child,
and sent her away;
***she went** and wandered in the wilderness of Beersheba.*

***She went** and sat down, facing him, at a distance*
of about a bowshot . . .

God opened her eyes and she saw:
a well of water!
***She went** and filled the container with water*
and gave the boy a drink.

Three times in this short passage Hagar "went," her movement carrying the plot along. The Hebrew word for "went" (*halak*) can be translated in many different ways depending on the context (go, walk, depart, leave; it can even mean to die or pass away). The flexibility of this common Hebrew word leads to a repetition and rhythm not altogether captured in translation.

Taken out of context, the first of these phrases might evoke, especially for those of us whose literary traditions are shaped by colonizing and conquest, a decision to strike out and explore the world. We know by now, however, that Hagar had no choice. Abraham and Sarah banished her, so she went and wandered about in an inhospitable wilderness. In the transition from slavery to wilderness, the scene changed dramatically, but her precarious position remained the same. The second occurrence of the phrase "she went" ushers in no great change of scenery but represents the great potential at this point in the story for a massive change in Ishmael and Hagar's circumstances. The final appearance of the phrase is a reversal of the first. Hagar remained in the wilderness, but the wilderness became a place where she and Ishmael could make their home (cf. vv. 20–21).

Seeing and Hearing (vv. 16–17, 19)

She went and sat down facing him,
at a distance of about a bowshot, saying,
"Do not let me see
the death of the child." So she sat facing him,
and she lifted up her voice and wept.
God heard
the voice of the boy, and a messenger from God called to Hagar
from the heavens and said to her, "What is the matter, Hagar?
Do not fear, for

God has heard the voice of the boy where he is.

God opened her eyes and
she saw:
a well of water! She went and filled the container with water
and gave the boy a drink.

The Old Testament is full of striking reversals of fortune, where enslaved Hebrew midwives outwit the pharaoh of a kingdom known for its wisdom, and prophetic voices proclaim a God who lifts up the poor to sit among princes (see Exodus 1:15–20; 1 Samuel 2:8). This instance is no less striking. Beginning with a situation so tragic that Hagar could not bear to look upon it, God opened Hagar's eyes to the means of their salvation. Nestled between these two references to sight, we are told that God heard Ishmael's cries. To many readers, the fact that God responded to *Ishmael's* and not Hagar's cries may be a surprise. We just witnessed the heart-rending scene through the eyes of the grieving mother, not the child. Yet Ishmael's cries—off-stage, so to speak—are the ones to which God responded.

We might spend some time pondering this detail. It may elicit a variety of responses leading to meaningful conversation about encountering the God of love. Having been drawn into Hagar's plight and told by our biblical narrator that Hagar "lifted her voice and wept," (v. 16), I was primed to expect God's messenger to declare, "I have heard *your* cry." I am troubled that, throughout her appearance in Genesis, so little attention is given to Hagar as a person whose own life matters. Here, however, God's attentions to the cries of the boy surround the simple question that the messenger put to Hagar as he called her by name, asking, "What is wrong?" (v. 17).

Perhaps Hagar responded to the voice from the heavens through gesture or words. She could have responded as Micah did, when such a question was posed to him: with angry incredulity, a brief summary of the present situation, followed with, "How can you ask me 'What is the matter'?" (Judges 18:23–24). Perhaps she simply continued weeping, like the elders of Jabesh who awaited someone to save them from a horrible fate (1 Samuel 11:2–5). The rest of the divine messenger's response shows that God was aware that Hagar's cries were caused by Ishmael's. God knew why she suffered, and in responding to Ishmael's cries, God answered Hagar's.

Encountering the God of Love in Genesis 21

At the outset of this biblical narrative, Hagar and Ishmael experienced anything but loving kindness from Abraham and Sarah. They used and abused Hagar (see especially Genesis 16:1–6) and then left her to a perilous fate.[4] Hagar did not encounter the God of love among the patriarch and matriarch of our faith. She encountered the God of love in the wilderness, in her moment of deepest need. Though Abraham and Sarah reduced her to these circumstances, God provided another avenue through which Hagar and Ishmael could survive. Though they spoke *about* Hagar, God spoke *to* her. They saw her only for how she could benefit or threaten them, while God provided her with a life of freedom.

Within this short passage, I find two powerful messages—one of hope and the other of biting condemnation. We rejoice that a child's life was spared, that cries of anguish were heard and needs met, and that God's love is made manifest by hearing and seeing our deepest pain. Yet, in this case, such divine love did *not* come through the recipients of God's great covenantal promise, Abraham and Sarah; it came in spite of them.

Interpreting the Symbolism

Having meditated on the repeated words and phrases in Genesis 21:14–19, we may carry the discussion of these themes beyond this

4. God's words to Abraham in 21:12–13 hardly exonerate Abraham of his behavior throughout. Nor does it benefit us as interpreters to excuse Abraham and Sarah for living in a time when slavery was an accepted practice. The Old Testament does not purport to present us with models of perfect living, nor should we fail to acknowledge wrongdoing in order to preserve our heroes of the faith.

particular passage. In some cases, I will highlight the symbolic power of an image as it is used elsewhere in the Bible. In others, I will consider how these symbols might have meaning in new contexts. As but one interpreter, my commentary will be limited to the insights of one biblical scholar interpreting theologically. I tend to identify with Abraham and Sarah rather than with Hagar and Ishmael. They are, of course, the patriarch and matriarch of God's covenantal people in the Old Testament, from whom Jesus arose, and into whose covenantal relationship with God Christians are grafted. There are ways in which I can identify with Hagar, but there are more ways in which I cannot—especially in her experience as a slave and fighting for her basic survival. In fact, I am aware that at least one of my ancestors was a slave *owner*. For this reason, it would be irresponsible of me to identify solely with Hagar in this story without also taking a hard look at Abraham, Sarah, and Isaac's role in the background of this story. In what follows, I interpret this passage in light of both its focus on Hagar and the role of Sarah and Abraham.

Seeing and Hearing the Truth before Us

The power of Hagar and Ishmael's encounter with God begins with the simple fact that God heard and acknowledged their pain. There are too many types of pain in this world that even those of us who consider ourselves ambassadors for God ignore. There is probably something to the fact that in this digital, global age, we are oversaturated with painful news. We simply cannot bear it all. But there are also times when we willfully close ourselves off to the cries of others because we cannot be burdened with participating in the path to justice, are afraid to let go of our privileges in order to extend loving mercy, and refuse to humble ourselves to acknowledge our own complicity when it stares us in the face. For those of us accustomed to being the bringers of good news, it can be humbling to acknowledge the messengers of God who expose our flaws.

As God followers, we can imitate God's love for us by opening our eyes and ears to the pain of others. Sometimes these cries are accompanied by eloquent theological reflection. Much of the time, they pour out in fits and starts. We can pray that God would give us ears to hear when we approach each other honestly with our pain. The holy power of listening deeply to one another cannot be overestimated. Conversely, the unholy power of judging harshly before listening deeply can do irreparable harm to our Christian witness. Doing so can communicate that the life of faith requires us to gloss over our deepest and most pressing concerns, and that God and God's church neither see nor hear.

Wandering in the Wilderness

Often in the Old Testament, especially in the books of the prophets, the word translated "wander" is used to describe leaders who led the people astray, meandering away from God (e.g., Isaiah 29:24; 53:6; Jeremiah 23:13; Amos 2:4; Micah 3:5). The most extended appearance of wilderness in the Bible is the Hebrew people's forty years of wandering in the wilderness after being freed from slavery in Egypt. That story of freedom from oppression was set in motion when God "saw" the people's hardship, "heard" their cries, and "knew" their sufferings (Exodus 3:7). Once freed, the people were dissatisfied with God's provision in the wilderness and longed to return to Egypt. They ended up wandering through the wilderness for forty years until a new generation arose to enter the promised land. As many a preacher knows, "wilderness" becomes a biblical symbol with which we discuss many theological topics. We may take care to note that wilderness can represent different realities and that people end up in the wilderness due to varying circumstances.

In Genesis 21, Hagar and Ishmael's wandering led them to an encounter with God. They did not choose to go astray; they were forced into the wilderness by the people of God who had received the promises of God yet who used Hagar and Ishmael to try to realize God's promises through their own means—and then cast them out when their presence was no longer convenient.[5] We do not always end up in the wilderness due to our own sin or faithlessness. Sometimes it is a result of others' actions. In light of this reality, we may consider the following two applications: (1) We ought not presume to know why someone is in a place of wilderness in their life, and (2) We may take hope that God sees and hears the cries of anyone who is in the wilderness.

Bearing Our Burdens

Perhaps the most heartrending moment of Hagar's story in Genesis 21 is the moment she cast down Ishmael under the bush. The image may invoke a number of responses for readers, ranging from sadness to shock, empathy, or revulsion. Whatever the response, it is likely to be a strong one. Her accompanying cry, "Do not let me see the death of the child," cemented the agony of the moment. Her gesture of "casting down" her child was symbolic of her laying down the burden she carried in her heart. It was not total; though she walked away, she did not abandon him completely. She gained the distance she needed to survive the anguish of the moment. But she could still see the place where she left him. So, having symbolically but not totally laid down her burden, she raised her voice and wept.

Those of us with deep roots in the Holiness tradition may be familiar with calls to lay down our burdens at an altar. Altars are places of surrender where we lay down our sins, our burdens—even our life plans—before the Lord. We cast down our burdens with our presence, our words, and our tears. Often, we have come to the end of ourselves, uncertain of what will happen but sharing the weight of the burden with God.

The symbolism of Hagar's story reminds us that the end of the story doesn't come when we grow weary from carrying our burdens. Nor are we solely responsible for the burdens we carry, even when

5. Sarah did not want to see Hagar's son, Ishmael, inherit from Abraham alongside her own son, Isaac (Genesis 21:10).

others, like Sarah and Abraham, have let us down. God still sees; God yet hears and heeds our cries. We can always lift up our honest petitions to God. And when we are too weary for words, God hears those prayers too.

In Search of Water

Hagar and Ishmael's needs were of the most basic kind: water, food, shelter. Those of us who are secure in these needs may need to reread Genesis 21 from the perspective of Sarah and Abraham, to ask God to show us ways in which we participate in the withholding of our goods to the detriment of others. Indeed, much of the Bible—the Old Testament as well as the New—instructs the people of God to care for the poor and those made most vulnerable in every society.

If we reread Genesis 21:14–21 for all its symbolic possibilities, the water for which we search may take on any number of forms in addition to having our physical needs met. Some of these we all share: the need for the waters of love, compassion, and acceptance from others and from the God who created us. Other forms that water takes will depend on our particular circumstances. Whatever the water stands for, we are incapable of supplying these needs entirely on our own. When such life-giving water runs dry in our lives, we bear the burden heavily. As our pain wends itself into our lives, we are, in essence, crying out, "Do not let me look upon this death" that comes from a lack of what we seek.

Note what it is that enacted the transformation from death to life in this biblical narrative. "God heard," and then "she saw" the water before her. Not only are readers told that God heard; Hagar herself was told by the messenger of God. This detail, however small, may have enormous significance in our interpretation. God did not skip over compassion on the way to a solution. God could have simply led her to the well, allowing her to assume that the water she found was merely a coincidence in an otherwise cruel world. Instead, God spoke to Hagar through a messenger, asked her what was wrong, and told her God had heard her cry. Perhaps once she had refreshed Ishmael and herself with water, she was further strengthened by reflecting on her extraordinary encounter with the divine.

Encountering the God of Love in Light of Genesis 21

There are two takeaways that arise out of this reading of Genesis 21:14–21. For some of us, only one message will apply more personally; others will see themselves in both. The first is a message of caution that leads us to ask God to reveal difficult truths and allow God to transform us more fully into God's likeness. Simply having a relationship with God does not mean everyone automatically experiences the love of God through us. Despite our best intentions, we can fail to love, fail to listen, and fail to acknowledge painful truths without simple solutions. Sometimes we push Hagars and Ishamels away, absolve ourselves of the difficulties they suffer, and still call ourselves the people of God.

The good news of the Holiness tradition is that the Spirit of God has the power to transform us further into the likeness of the God of love. Sanctification extends beyond a first moment at an altar. The indwelling of the Holy Spirit remains with us along our journeys of faith. By remaining in a prayerful posture of consecration to God's will, we invite the Spirit to reveal to us aspects of ourselves and our communities that are in need of transformation. Such revelation can come directly from cries in the wilderness. By listening, loving, and acknowledging painful truths, we not only extend the love of God to others, but we also allow God to begin the necessary work among us to participate in the path to healing.

The second message of good news is that God met with Hagar and Ishmael in the wilderness. When we have been dismissed, pushed out, or deeply wronged—even by the church—the creative Spirit of God can show up wherever we are. The burdens we carry are real and lamentable, especially when those who have hurt us deny they did anything wrong. It is equally true that God's story does not end when some of God's people fail. God still loves us, even as we ache to experience that love from people who worship God. God still values us even if we begin to question our own value. And we can look for those messengers of God who ask us what is wrong, who listen, and who love us as we wait together for God to show us the way to the life-giving water we need.

Questions for Discussion

1. When have you experienced the love of God in a time of wilderness? Were there messengers of God who shared divine love with you?
2. In what circumstances do you or your church community need courage from God to listen deeply to the cries of others?
3. What kinds of cries do those in positions of influence in your church community seem unwilling to hear?
4. Who will be the messengers of God who will acknowledge these cries in order to express God's love?
5. Where is God at work, providing and loving, even beyond your local church community?

2. SHOW ME YOUR GLORY, I PRAY

EXODUS 33:12–34:10

TIMOTHY M. GREEN

Describing the Indescribable: Moses's Bold Request

Of all the prayers recorded in the Bible, one of the boldest is Moses's request to the LORD, "Show me your glory!" (Exodus 33:18).[1] Across the millennia, the word "glory" has become so commonplace in the songs, prayers, sermons, and testimonies of God's people that we are at risk of being unaware of this word's unique meaning, or of redefining its meaning altogether. In order to discover the significance of Moses's request and its profound impact on our understanding of the LORD, particularly as portrayed in the Old Testament, I will explore the narrative in which Moses makes the request. This narrative is actually embedded within a much larger context, beginning with the meticulous guidelines given by God to Moses for the construction of the tabernacle, and ending with the people's departure from Sinai.

However, before we begin our journey through this passage, let's briefly examine the way our biblical ancestors understood the LORD's glory. Have you ever attempted to describe the indescribable or explain the unexplainable? Words are inadequate, and graphic pictures fall short. Our biblical ancestors faced this quandary as they encountered the LORD's unique presence in their lives. While they could and did confess the LORD's promise to barren and landless ancestors, the mighty acts of deliverance from Egypt and provision in the wilderness, and the covenant at Sinai, these testimonies were not adequate in describing the unique character of the LORD God who was present with them.

In order to describe the general idea of uniqueness or set-apartness from all other divine and human powers, our biblical ancestors had access to an adjective they frequently used. We often translate that adjective as "holy." This word appears often in our ancestors' songs and testimonies to describe the reality that nothing else compared to the LORD their God. The LORD was completely different,

1. All translations are the author's unless otherwise noted.

separate, one of a kind. From the seraphim chorus in Isaiah 6:3, "Holy, Holy, Holy is the LORD of hosts," to the hymn in Psalm 99, "Magnify the LORD our God . . . because the LORD our God is holy," our ancestors were convinced that the LORD was uniquely set apart from all other powers. As significant and useful as this adjective was in the Israelites' vocabulary, it simply pointed to the reality that the LORD was distinct from all divine and earthly powers, but it did not specify exactly *what* was unique in the LORD's character and nature.

So the quandary continues. Is there any concrete way of depicting the LORD's distinct character as the LORD is present with the chosen people? Is there an image to see, a sound to hear, an object to touch, that might reflect the LORD's holy presence among the people without that image becoming a religious means (i.e., an idol) to domesticate or manipulate God's presence? The priestly community who instructed our ancestors in the ways of the LORD would respond, "Yes, indeed, there is just such an image; it is the glory of the LORD." At the heart of the Hebrew word (*kabod*) often translated "glory" is the literal meaning of heaviness, or weightiness, such as we see in the description of the heavy priest Eli (1 Samuel 4:18), or of Absalom's weighty hair (2 Samuel 14:26). However, this literal meaning of weightiness acquires a more figurative meaning as it depicts one in a community whose identity and presence carry weight. That person's honorable position evokes the community's respect. We see this notion in the command to give honor (literally, "glory") to one's parents (Exodus 20:12). It often appears in acclamations of worship such as, "The LORD of hosts is the king of glory" (Psalm 24:10); or, "I will glorify your name forever" (Psalm 86:12, NRSV). Ultimately the people apply this more abstract notion of divine honor or glory to a concrete, observable reality: the LORD is present with the people so that the physical manifestation of God's glorious presence appears in the form of a brilliant light or consuming fire.

Earlier in Exodus, the presence of the LORD appeared to Moses in the form of an unquenchable fire at the burning bush (3:2–6) and to the whole community in the form of fire and cloud (13:21–22). Once Moses ascended Sinai in 24:15–18, the text specifically names the blazing fire within the cloud as "the glory of the LORD" (v. 17, NIV) and describes it not as permanently dwelling on the mountain but as "tabernacling" (using the same root as the word for tabernacle)—taking up temporary residence on the mountain. In the final verses of the book of Exodus (40:34–38), the fire and cloud again appear as the LORD's glory descended from the mountain and filled the tabernacle and the LORD prepared to sojourn with the people toward the promised land.

Israel's covenant God was simply living up to the unique meaning of the personal name "YHWH." Just as the LORD had promised to be present with Moses *wherever* Moses would go, the LORD's sojourning presence would now go with the community through the wilderness and into the land of promise. It is no wonder, then, that when King David desired to build a permanent house (temple) for the LORD, God responded, "I have not lived in a house since the day I brought up the people of Israel from Egypt to this day, but I have been moving about in a tent and a tabernacle" (2 Samuel 7:6, NRSV). As the LORD's unique presence journeyed with the covenant community, they literally became the bearers, or carriers, of the LORD's unique character (i.e., the glory) among the nations.

Even this remarkable manifestation of the LORD's glorious presence does not communicate precisely what is so unique about the LORD. It simply continues to call the people to honor, revere, and worship the LORD as their holy God. Whether subsequent generations testified to the mighty acts of God, joined the heavenly beings in singing, "Holy, holy, holy," or prayed for the LORD's glory to shine upon them, they were still left asking, "What is the unique, honor-evoking character of the one who stands behind the mighty acts, the holy language, and the fiery glory?"

Such odd, even frightening, language might leave worshipers shaking in terror at the presence of this holy God in the same way that Dorothy and her three companions stood before the oversized green face of the Wizard of Oz. Making himself known to these four terrified characters through a flaming fire and rising smoke, the unknowable and unapproachable wizard exclaimed, "I am Oz, the great and powerful. Who are you? Who are you?"

Dorothy simply replied, "I am Dorothy, the small and meek."

Left to our own imaginations, we begin to give definition to the LORD's glory-bearing uniqueness based on our own preconceived notions of deity, sovereignty, power, glory, and holiness. Misconceptions that we may bring to the perplexing and often cryptic language of the LORD's glory unintentionally contribute to widespread misunderstandings of God in the Old Testament as a Wizard-of-Oz-like power who stands frighteningly apart from humanity and whose terrorizing wrath stands ready to burst open at any moment.

In Exodus 33, Moses steps into the throne room not of a fictitious, green-faced wizard but of Israel's mighty deliverer, provider, and covenant partner. With the boldness and faith of one to whom God spoke as "a friend" (Exodus 33:11), Moses courageously yet reverently requested, "Show me your glory, I pray!" (v. 18). At the heart of his request was the desire to know the nature and the ways, the character and the practices, of the one who stood behind the fiery glory.

The Context of Moses's Request

Moses's request occurs within two specific contexts. The first context is comprised of the meticulous instructions for the tabernacle (Exodus 25–31) and the people's obedient construction of the tabernacle (Exodus 35–40). Between these lengthy passages is the narrative that includes Moses's request to see the LORD's glory (Exodus 32–34). The LORD's glorious presence that sojourns with the people as they carry the tabernacle through the wilderness demonstrates the integral relationship between covenant God and covenant people. To encounter the covenant community is to encounter the unique nature and character of the LORD. As the tabernacling presence of the LORD journeys with the covenant people, they become the bearers of the divine uniqueness. In light of this integral relationship between the two covenant partners, the LORD will call the people to be holy (set apart) simply because the LORD is holy (see Leviticus 19:2).

The second context of Moses's request in 33:18 is the full narrative in chapters 32–34, which appears at first sight to be an abrupt interruption of the tabernacle instructions and construction. However, this three-chapter narrative sets the stage for what will be the great dilemma of God's people throughout all time—their repeated failure to be faithful in carrying out their end of the covenant relationship with the LORD. Having grown impatient for Moses's return while he was on Mount Sinai, the people requested Aaron to make a god (an idol) who would continue the journey with them. As Aaron willingly participated in the people's rebellion and shaped the image of a calf, the community responded, "These are your gods, O Israel, who brought you up out of the land of Egypt!" (Exodus 32:4). In turn, Aaron constructed an altar and announced that there would be a feast in honor of the LORD on the following day. The actions of both Aaron and the people were not carried out in the name of another deity but in the name of their covenant God, YHWH.

This incident was not the last time the LORD's people would construct idols. This idolatrous tendency to domesticate and manipulate the LORD through the misuse of the divine name and the construction of idols has characterized the LORD's covenant people throughout the history of the community. Even in chapters 32–34, the people's idolatry was certainly more than the simplistic act of designing a statue. It was the ultimate act of infidelity in which the LORD's people broke covenant relationship that the LORD established only a few chapters earlier (see chapter 19).

Observing that God "cannot, he will not, quit his claim, or consent to [our heart's] being given to any other," John Wesley described idolatry as the act of giving "our heart to any other" so that "whatever takes our heart from him, or shares it with him is an idol."[2] Describing idolatry as the central covenantal offense against the LORD, J. Gerald Janzen has indicated that the deeper problem underlying idolatry is trust (or lack of trust) in the LORD. Janzen observes that "more grave than the lack of obedience is the lack of trust. Not seeing what provision God has made behind the scenes for their welfare . . . Israel at Mount Sinai act[s] out of anxiety to provide for their own well-being." He concludes that "where God's trust does not win answering trust, the sort of relation into which God seeks to draw us is not possible."[3]

Aware of the covenantal crisis that was taking place at the base of the mountain in chapter 32, the LORD insisted that Moses go down to "*your* people whom *you* brought up out of the land of Egypt" (v. 7, emphasis added). Describing the covenant people as a perverse, stiff-necked (i.e., stubbornly rebellious) community who quickly turned aside from God's ways, the LORD concluded that a great nation would now be made only from Moses and not from this people. Using the very words that the LORD used in referring to the Israelites, Moses responded to the LORD by arguing that these people were "*your* people whom *you* brought out of the land of Egypt" (v. 11, emphasis added). The dialogue reveals a tense moment in which neither the LORD nor Moses wanted to claim the people as their own. Reminding the LORD of the promise to the ancestors, Moses pleaded for the LORD not to abandon the covenant community.

How ironic that, after Moses's urgent plea for the LORD to spare the people and the LORD's agreement (v. 14), Moses himself became so infuriated when he heard the festive noises and saw the frivolity of the people that he broke the original tablets into pieces as he threw them to the ground (v. 19). The very symbol of the covenant between

---

2. John Wesley, *The Works of John Wesley*, vol. 3, ed. Albert C. Outler (Nashville: Abingdon, 1986), 104–105.

3. J. Gerald Janzen, *Exodus*, *Westminster Bible Companion* (Louisville: Westminster John Knox Press, 1997), 230.

the LORD and the people was shattered. Nevertheless, Moses continued to implore the LORD to forgive the covenant people. Meeting Moses halfway, the LORD agreed to Moses's taking the people into the land of promise, but the LORD would no longer journey with them since their "stiff-necked" nature would only bring about their demise (33:1–13).

These two narratives—the tabernacle's construction (chapters 25–31; 35–40) and the community's rebellion (chapters 32–34)—provide the two-part context in which Moses's request to see the LORD's glory appears. Tabernacle versus Rebellion: there appears to be no resolution. On one hand, the covenant community was meant to carry the tabernacling presence of God, embodied in the glory, with them on their journey. On the other hand, the people's covenant-making God forsook the covenant-rebelling people and thus could not continue to accompany them on the journey. In the midst of the impasse, the heart of the LORD's prophet and the people's shepherd, Moses, was torn between the God who called him and the people to whom he was called. The God-forsaken covenant community was left only with the residual shame, wounds, and hopelessness of their offense against God.

Is there any hope for resolution? Is reconciliation between the rebellious, glory-bearing community and their glorious God even a remote possibility? Does the story of a forsaken God, a torn leader, and a called but rebellious people end at an impasse? Is the LORD's character one that will move both the LORD and the people beyond the past to bring healing to the present and to journey together into the future? Or does humanity have to wait another thirteen centuries before they encounter a God with a loving nature and character?

The Glory Passes By

Moses has certainly not been a passive figure up to this point, and he does not become one now as he pushes his dialogue with the LORD even further beginning in Exodus 33:12: "You've not let me know whom you will send with me even though you said, 'I know you by name, and you have found grace before my eyes.'" Affirming the integral relationship between covenant God and covenant people, Moses was insistent that, if the LORD went no farther with them, there was no reason for Moses or the community to proceed at all, since the only thing that set them apart from other communities was God's unique presence.

Moses pushed further, "If I have found grace in your eyes, let me know your ways [i.e., the paths that you take] so that I may know you" (v. 13). What a remarkable request! In order for Moses to "know" the LORD, the LORD must let Moses "know" the divine ways. The dialogue finally reached its climax as Moses prayed, "Show me your glory!" (v. 18). Terence Fretheim has described this request as Moses's desire "to see God's very self."[4] He essentially asked, "What stands behind the enigmatic, honorable, holy, blazing fire that we call your glory? What ways separate and distinguish you from all other divine and human powers? Who are you—really?"

Rather than belittling or denying Moses's emphatic request, the Lord affirmed first that the creating and life-giving divine goodness would pass by Moses (v. 19). The LORD would once again call out the divine name previously revealed at the burning bush, YHWH (3:13–15). Inherent within the LORD's life-giving goodness and name are the very ways (the character and practices) of the LORD that Moses so desired to know. Although the LORD's name itself would be nothing new to Moses, this time the LORD would follow that name with divine words that revealed the unique nature and character of the covenant God. As is the case with all human beings, Moses would not be able to observe or predict the LORD's coming ("you cannot see my face," 33:20), but he would undoubtedly know once the LORD's presence had come ("you will see my back," v. 23). Anticipating the

4. Terence E. Fretheim, *Exodus*, *Interpretation: A Bible Commentary for Teaching and Preaching* (Louisville: Westminster John Knox Press, 1991), 299.

consequences of the LORD's glorious presence, Moses prepared two stones to replace the two he shattered. Is it possible that a story of infidelity, forsakenness, disappointment, and hopelessness could end in faithfulness, forgiveness, restoration, and hope?

In the climactic moment of the narrative, the LORD's glorious presence passed by Moses (34:5–6). The words that follow the twice-repeated divine name, "YHWH, YHWH," describe the nature and character that stand behind the LORD's name and glory. By means of adjectives, the LORD pulled back the mysterious curtain that concealed the nature of God's glory. What Moses witnessed was no aloof, Wizard-of-Oz-like power who sat on the edge of the divine seat, waiting to unleash destructive wrath and terror. Actually, the descriptive words all depict a relational being: merciful toward *the other*, gracious toward *the other,* slow to anger toward *the other*, faithful toward *the other*, and forgiving of *the other* (34:6–7). Because each adjective assumes that the LORD is relational to others, to remove a relational partner would be to nullify the meaning of each word that the LORD speaks. No adjective is an isolated, self-contained characteristic of God. As the glory passed, one could legitimately repeat the previous announcement: "Here, O Israel, is your God who brought you up out of the land of Egypt!" (32:4). However, a great chasm existed between the LORD's glory and the Israelites' idol: the first is a relational being; the second was not.

Emerging from one's deepest inner being, the first adjective used to describe the LORD in 34:6 is often translated as "merciful" or "compassionate." A related form of this word denotes a mother's womb that provides protection, nourishment, and intimate care to the unborn child who is unable to care for itself. This merciful nature often depicts a more powerful individual's life-giving action toward a weaker or more vulnerable individual, such as a mother to a nursing infant (Isaiah 49:15) or a father to a young child (Psalm 103:13). The adjective stands in direct contrast to power that is used to threaten and destroy another. The LORD is merciful!

The second adjective in Exodus 34:6, often translated as "gracious," depicts unearned favor toward another through life-giving actions without prerequisites. Because it seeks nothing in return for life-giving actions, it freely extends deliverance and provision, restoration and forgiveness. The word often appears in the Bible to describe relationships between two people, such as Potiphar and Joseph (Genesis 39:4); Ruth and Boaz (Ruth 2:13); and David and Jonathan (1 Samuel 20:3). In the LORD's relationship with human beings, this graciousness emerges solely from the LORD's character and not from human performance or achievement. Although human beings are recipients of divine graciousness, the term emphasizes the nature of God as giver rather than the human as recipient. The LORD is gracious!

Comprising two words literally translated as "long (of) nose," the third adjective in Exodus 34:6 is a Hebrew idiom for "slow to anger." This idiom assumes knowledge of a related one for anger, "heat (flaring up) of nostrils" (see 32:10). Rather than having nostrils that flare up quickly, the LORD's anger, or wrath, is a long, drawn-out process. To use a closely related idiom in English, the LORD is not hot-tempered or short-tempered. In contrast to destructive human anger, the LORD does not become easily exasperated, bursting forth in a fit of rage without thought or compassion. Whatever divine anger is present is couched within the context of God's mercy and graciousness on one end and God's faithfulness and forgiveness on the other end. The LORD is slow to anger!

The fourth phrase in 34:6, composed of three words, is literally translated as "much faithfulness and truth." While English Bibles translate the central word in a variety of ways, such as "steadfast love," "kindness," "loving kindness," or "grace," these translations fail to convey an essential matter regarding the already existing relationship between the LORD and the people—namely, the covenant. Within that all-important context, this word is more appropriately translated as "covenant faithfulness (fidelity)." The term conveys the affirmation that when the LORD has said, "I do" to a people, the

LORD remains true to that vow. This covenant God does not abruptly abandon the covenant people but consistently remains loyal and faithful to them. Because covenant faithfulness was to be a two-way street between the LORD and the community, the people of God were likewise to be faithful to the LORD. Unfortunately, they regularly struggled with faithfulness. In fact, the eighth-century-BCE prophet Hosea compared the people's covenant faithfulness to morning dew that appears momentarily but quickly evaporates (Hosea 6:4). In contrast to the people's fickle fidelity, the LORD does not give up on them in spite of their offenses.

The third word in this three-word phrase referring to covenant faithfulness literally means "truth." While it may simply serve as a synonym for covenant faithfulness (thus, faithfulness and truthfulness), it very likely modifies or further describes the second word, so that the nature of God's covenant faithfulness is truthful, honest, or consistent—what Walter Brueggemann has called "complete reliability."[5] As if the second and third words were not enough, the text adds an adjective on the front end—"many," or "much"—in order to depict that the LORD's "consistent faithfulness" is abundant or overflowing. The LORD is overflowing with covenant faithfulness!

As the word for "covenant faithfulness" reappears at the beginning of verse 7, the fifth phrase continues the focus upon the LORD's fidelity. In this instance, however, the emphasis is upon the manner in which the LORD continually (in an ongoing action) watches over covenant faithfulness in the same way that a guard at a military post or a lookout in an agricultural field keeps an alert eye for any intruders or threats. In the same way, the LORD keeps a watchful and protective eye on the divine covenant faithfulness. The protection of the LORD's fidelity does not merely last up to the thousandth generation

5. Walter Brueggemann, "The Book of Exodus" in *The New Interpreter's Bible: General & Old Testament Articles, Genesis, Exodus, Leviticus*, vol. 1, ed. Walter Brueggemann, Walter C. Kaiser, Leander E. Keck, and Terence E. Fretheim (Nashville: Abingdon Press, 1994), 946.

but literally for thousands of generations. In other words, it never comes to an end. As the psalmist often celebrates, "His covenant faithfulness endures forever" (Psalms 100:5; 118; 136). The LORD IS watching over covenant faithfulness to the very end!

The sixth and final descriptor in Exodus 34:6–7 serves as the culmination to the passing by of the LORD's glory. Taken together, the preceding five descriptors engender the ultimate goal or end of our passage: divine forgiveness. Although we appropriately translate the word in verse 7 as "forgiving," it literally means "to lift off" or "to take up." God's forgiving character is not simply an internalized mental repression of human offense. Neither is it embodied in the superficial words of a God who half-heartedly says, "Don't worry; I forgive you." In fact, the very notion of God's "lifting off" something from a person or a community emphasizes less about the impact on God and more about the impact on the human being. Brueggemann has described the essence of this word as the act of relieving "covenant violators of the burden of their violation."[6] The actions or practices that have weighed heavily upon the offender and that have likely brought alienation, shame, fear, exclusion, paralysis, and despair have been "lifted off" not by the offender but by the one against whom the offense was carried out.

What offenses does the LORD "lift off" of human beings? Verse 7 uses the three primary terms that appear in the Old Testament to describe an offense against God or against one's neighbor (see all three in Psalm 51:1–5). Each term conveys a unique nuance regarding the offense. The first term often appears in English translations as "iniquity" (NIV, "wickedness"). Rather than being a mere synonym for sin, this word reflects both the offense and its residual effect. While this term can be appropriately translated as "guilt" or "shame," we should be careful not to limit it to an internalized personal emotion, since it often has multiple interpersonal and societal ramifications.

6. Brueggemann, "The Book of Exodus," 946.

We can compare the term to the person who walks in mud and, as a result, has muddy feet. Two issues are at stake: the offense of walking in mud and the aftereffect of muddy feet. The word "iniquity" attempts to communicate both. The term itself is not concerned with the offender's intentions but with the act itself and the act's associated aftereffects.

The second term is often translated into English as "transgression." Emphasizing the intentions of an offender, this term depicts an offense that one has knowingly and purposefully carried out. We can compare this term to walking over a clearly marked line deliberately. The one who walks over the line sees the line in advance and is aware when she or he has crossed over it. This term emphasizes the conscious and intentional nature of an offense.

The final term is commonly translated into English as the more generic word "sin." It essentially conveys any act that misses a target or goal, regardless of intentionality. As the offender becomes aware of missing a designated mark, she or he is responsible for any necessary reparations. We can compare the essence of this word with the sport of archery. While the target is obvious to the archer, the archer may miss the target by accident or on purpose. The emphasis of this term is not so much upon intent (as with transgression) or aftereffect (as with iniquity) but more on the actual act of missing the target.

While it may be enticing to turn the various words in verses 6–7 into separate bullet points and study them individually, these words do not function in isolation from one another. Rather, as a whole entity, they culminate in the LORD's "lifting off" every knowable type of offense against God and neighbor. Taken together, they define the LORD's character: mercy-extending graciousness that is not easily angered but remains consistently and abundantly faithful to all generations. The end of this glorious character finds its expression in a distinct form of life and practice: forgiveness and restoration. This kind of forgiveness is not simply a divinely internalized act in which the LORD "feels better" toward offenders but is an act that directly affects the offenders, whose offenses are "lifted off" their life and identity.

The sudden shift in tone in the middle of verse 7 should not cause us to stop reading the text in order to avoid what appears to be a difficult matter in light of the LORD's forgiveness. The latter half of verse 7 is not an alternative, contradiction, or afterthought to what the text has already said regarding forgiveness. Rather, it is a continuation that attempts to clarify the nature of the LORD's forgiveness. Forgiveness is neither divine manipulation nor magic in which the LORD obliterates the aftereffects of the actions of a generation, community, or individual. Human offenses against God, humanity, and creation can and often do result, on an ongoing basis, in unhealthy or destroyed relationships, wounded bodies and minds, life-threatening political, economic, and religious systems, fractured societies, and deteriorating created order. Others who have not participated in an offense may yet experience the consequence of another's offense. To think and speak otherwise would be to deceive ourselves and others, as well as to believe in and perpetuate a falsehood about both God's forgiveness and forgiven human beings.

Unfortunately, the second half of verse 7 has been understood and even translated in an erroneous, nonbiblical way that ends up nullifying all that has been stated regarding God's mercy, grace, faithfulness, and forgiveness. Even the word "yet" added by many translations at the beginning of the second half of verse 7 (which does not appear in the Hebrew text) inappropriately conveys that what follows is a contrast to what has preceded. As a result of erroneous understandings and translations, the LORD appears to carry out arbitrary punishments upon innocent descendants of guilty generations. However, in the statement that the LORD does not "clear the guilty," the word "forgive" does not appear. This line has absolutely nothing to do with God's forgiveness, nor does it depict the LORD as carrying a grudge that ultimately unloads delayed punishment on a later generation, another community, or an innocent individual.

The word instead depicts an action in which one exempts another from responsibility or obligations of their actions. This statement describes in an honest way the manner in which the LORD's forgiveness does not nullify ramifications or aftereffects of one's offenses. Likewise, in the line "punishing the sin," the term translated by some as "punishing" is literally "visiting," and that which is visited is not the sin or the transgression but the iniquity—or, as we have discussed previously—the residual effect of an offense.

In light of the LORD's forgiveness of every imaginable type of offense described in the first half of verse 7, these statements attempt to address the LORD's refusal to manipulate human beings in such a way that erases potential aftereffects or consequences that one generation may set into motion for subsequent generations. In light of God's unlimited forgiveness, these statements are a candid attempt to be true to life. On one hand, the aftereffects of a previous generation's actions upon the next generation in no way indicate the LORD's lack of forgiveness toward either generation. On the other hand, what one generation does matters for the next. Children and grandchildren inherit not only biological genes but also the effects of preceding generations' actions. The life-taking practices, habits, prejudices, fears, anger, and ways of viewing God, other human beings, and all creation continue to live on past any given generation.

So how do we receive and respond to this understanding of both divine and human forgiveness? The honesty of this passage first challenges the people of God in every generation to open our hearts and lives, our imagination and hope, our communities and ministries to discovering and implementing ways in which we can become authentic vessels of divine grace, wisdom, healing, and restoration to persons who have been directly affected by destructive and life-taking practices, including former generations.

Second, this passage's uncensored recognition of the effects of one generation upon another challenges the people of God honestly to see, to confess, and to remedy any life-taking ways and destructive practices we may be passing on to subsequent generations.

Finally, this passage's truth-telling about the generations challenges the people of God to be truth-tellers as we handle this passage with understanding, care, and wisdom, refusing to perpetuate any form of the falsehood that the LORD punishes one generation, one community, or one individual for the offenses of another. Indeed, sacred Scripture provides a radical alternative in a God whose mercy, grace, slowness to anger, covenant faithfulness, and forgiveness open the door to a tomorrow where all things become new.

The Backside of the Glory: Forgiveness and Restoration

Once God's glory passed by Moses, a divinely forgiven community lay in its wake. Indeed, Moses saw the "backside" of God (33:23). However, there was life beyond forgiveness. The ultimate end, or purpose, of the LORD's forgiveness is restoration, transformation, and a future in which God's people no longer live in the shadow of shame, fear, anxiety, abandonment, and despair. So as our ancestors left Sinai as God's forgiven children, forgiveness looked like two brand-new tablets to replace the ones shattered by Moses. It looked like a human leader who refused to set himself over against his people but placed himself as one with his people as he prayed that the LORD would pardon *our* iniquity and *our* sin and "take *us* as your inheritance" (34:9). It looked like a once threatened covenant that became new as the LORD announced, "Look! I am making a covenant" (v. 10). It looked like a God and God's divinely called leader who refused to give up on God's people, the world, and creation itself. It looked like the LORD's announcement of the unimaginable: "I will do marvelous things *which have not been created* on all the earth or in all the nations" (v. 10, emphasis added). Using the unique language that echoes Genesis 1:1, the LORD announced an utter transformation—a new creation—of all things. Describing this divine action as "an act parallel to the creation of the world,"

Fretheim states that "this act is of such an unprecedented nature that only creation language . . . can adequately describe it."[7] Ultimately, God's merciful, gracious, faithful, forgiving, and creating activity looks like the act of a God of love who is patient, kind, rejoicing in truth, bearing all things, trusting all things, hoping for all things, enduring all things. It looks like a God who never fails—a God, then, of love (see 1 Corinthians 13:4–8a).

Is it possible that the glory of God as depicted in Exodus 34 would be offensive for some who hear this text? Absolutely. Although we human beings are created in the image of God, our falling short of God's glory (Romans 3:23) leads us to create our own reality of glory and then apply that reality to God. Speaking of this very common practice, Paul wrote that we humans exchange "the glory of the immortal God for images resembling a mortal human being" (Romans 1:23). Creating our own definitions of sovereignty, power, holiness, justice, wrath, punishment, and forgiveness, we proceed to shape the LORD's image into our own image so that we no longer reflect the glory of God but create a god who reflects our definition of glory. As Brueggemann remarks, our unique covenant God "is not to be confused with or thought parallel to the insatiable gods of imperial productivity. This God is . . . revealed as a God of mercy, steadfast love, and faithfulness who is committed to covenantal relationships of fidelity."[8]

And the Glory Continues

The God who unites the Old and New Testaments continued and continues to call subsequent generations back to the "cleft of the rock" (Exodus 33:22), where God's people can again see the unique divine character as God's glory is revealed. It is certainly not by ac-

7. Fretheim, *Exodus*, 308.

8. Walter Brueggemann, *Sabbath as Resistance: Saying No to the Culture of Now* (Louisville: Westminster John Knox Press, 2014), 5–6.

cident that the Old Testament repeatedly returns to the confession of God's glory in Exodus 34:6–7. That confession finds its home in new generations, new contexts, and new forms. It is revealing that this confession of the LORD's character is the most-often-repeated passage through all of Scripture, appearing in multiple biblical time periods, genres, and contexts. That which Moses encountered was neither a one-time event nor a momentary interruption in God's character. As generations came and went, as mighty empires rose and fell, this glorious character of the LORD remained consistent in a creedal-like statement that appears in narratives, psalms, prayers, and prophets. Likewise, it consistently finds its place in contexts of divine forgiveness, restoration, and hope.

As the Hebrew spies returned from the land of promise and gave the discouraging report that giants dwelt in the land, the people of God rebelled (Numbers 14:1–25). When it appeared that the people of God had tightly slammed the door on the fulfillment of God's promise so that all hope was gone, the creedal statement of God's glory reappeared, opening the door to fulfilled promise.

As the generations following exile were attempting to rediscover their identity through proper worship and obedience to the LORD's instruction, Ezra rehearsed the LORD's faithfulness to all generations through a magnificent prayer (Nehemiah 9:6–37). As the prayer rehearsed the wilderness generation's grumbling and idolatry, the creedal statement of God's glory once again emerged on center stage. Indeed, because of the great divine mercies, the LORD did not abandon the people in the wilderness and would likewise remain faithful in the midst of new challenges.

In an undesignated time period in which locusts plagued and armies threatened the people of God, the prophet Joel reached deep into Israel's memory and brought the creedal statement of the LORD's glory to the surface once again. Calling upon the people in their fear and anxiety to turn to the Lord, Joel held open the possibility for divine blessing in light of the LORD's mercy and grace (Joel 2:12–14).

Opening and closing the timeless hymn with that great declaration, "Bless the LORD, O my soul," the psalmist articulated the manner in which the LORD had "made known his ways to Moses" (Psalm 103). Reclaiming the creedal confession of divine glory for the audience's own day, the psalmist applied this ancient creed by affirming that the LORD does not treat us according to our sins or pay us back for our iniquities. Rather, because the LORD's covenant faithfulness is as high as heaven is above the earth, so the LORD removes our sins from us as far as the east is from the west.

Of all the Old Testament passages in which this creedal confession from Exodus 34:6–7 appears, the one that turned the covenant community's preconceived world upside down was the narrative of Jonah. Protesting the LORD's command to preach to Israel's archenemy, Nineveh, the prophet became one of those persons easily offended by the LORD's glorious nature when he became a firsthand witness to Nineveh's repentance and the LORD's forgiveness. While all other creedal statements of the LORD's glory were within the context of God and the covenant family, Jonah came to the profound realization that, if this confession actually spoke of God's nature and character and not merely some sectarian personality, then it must also apply to the greatest enemies of God's people. Fleeing in the opposite direction of Nineveh, Jonah just could not extend a word of divine mercy and forgiveness to his enemy. However, in the end, he could do nothing but confess the essential character of the God of all creation: "I knew that you are a gracious God and merciful, slow to anger, and abounding in steadfast love" (Jonah 4:2, NRSV). Indeed, this glorious, forgiving love of God extends to all creation without boundaries.

The ongoing confession of the LORD's glory found in Exodus 34:6–7, however, does not end with these Old Testament texts. As the LORD's people have always recognized, the story of God must continue. It is appropriate for us to pause and imagine the great "what if?" in that continuing story. What if this brilliant glory that tabernacled with God's people would put on flesh and blood? What would the glory look like? What if the very essence of the divine glory—mercy, grace, slowness to anger, abundant faithfulness, and forgiveness of every imaginable offense—would appear as a living human being? How would that human being embody those attributes? What would that human being say? Where would that human being go? To whom would that human being extend mercy, grace, faithfulness, and forgiveness? In light of our looking back on the ongoing story of God, we respond to these "what if" questions by confessing that perhaps it is not necessary for us to imagine what the glory in human form would look like. We've seen with our eyes, heard with our ears, and touched with our hands the glory of God in the flesh. The divine glory indeed has become flesh and blood and has literally tabernacled among us so that we have "seen his glory, the glory as of a father's only son, full of grace and truth" (John 1:14, NRSV). Looking back upon the continuing story of God, Christians confess that the divine glory in flesh and blood is the son of Adam, the Son of God, Jesus Christ (see Luke 3:38).

However, even that story of the LORD's glory did not reach its conclusion two millennia ago. It continues as we live into God's future because that glorious future is breaking in upon us even now. Just as Moses's face shined so brightly with the LORD's glory that he had to put a veil over his face to protect the people from his own glow (Exodus 34:29–35), so all of us are "seeing with unveiled faces the LORD's glory as if we were looking into a mirror, so that we ourselves now are being transformed into that very image from glory into glory" (2 Corinthians 3:18).

As the story of God's glory and its tabernacling presence with God's people continues, perhaps the most significant question that we must continue to ask is, "What does the divine glory look like in flesh and blood?" The new covenant community that confesses that we have seen the LORD's glory in flesh and blood is itself the glory-bearing people of God in the world and in creation. How the LORD's covenant community perceives the divine glory undoubtedly shapes our relationship with God, each other, the world, and all creation. How we understand the LORD's unique nature—or holiness—directly impacts how we embody that unique nature in our day-to-day practices. As we are embraced by the glory of the LORD—mercy, grace, slowness to anger, abundant steadfast love, forgiveness of every type of offense—we become by grace what God is by nature. We come to recognize that the very essence of God's glory—God's holy love—is not found in internalized, abstract qualities but is always embodied in relationships—with God, each other, humanity, and all creation. The good news is that we no longer have to go and make up our own definition of divine glory. The sacred story that shapes us speaks into our lives and shows us what the glory looks like. The sacred Word that became flesh and dwelt among us has embodied that glory in his broken body and shed blood.

Ironically, we arrive back where we began—echoing the bold and transformational prayer of Moses, "Show us your glory, we pray." However, that prayer is not merely the request of a biblical hero. It has become our prayer too, and for us authentically to embody that prayer in our world, we continue it with these words: "and show the world your glory through us, we pray. Amen."

Questions for Discussion

1. In the past, when you have read, heard, or sung about God's glory, what thoughts and images came to your mind? Where do you believe those ideas came from?

2. Scripture indicates that the Lord's glory is mercy, grace, slowness to anger, abundant covenant faithfulness, faithfulness that has no end (to thousands of generations), and forgiving every type of sin. How does that characterization affect your understanding of and your relationship with God? How do you respond to this biblical depiction of God?

3. As you are being transformed from glory into glory, how is God inviting you to become by grace what God is by nature?
   a. In mercy to others?
   b. In graciousness toward others?
   c. In slowness to anger toward others?
   d. In covenant faithfulness with others?
   e. In forgiveness of others?

Bibliography

Brueggemann, Walter. "The Book of Exodus" in *The New Interpreter's Bible: General & Old Testament Articles, Genesis, Exodus, Leviticus*, vol. 1. Edited by Walter Brueggemann, Walter C. Kaiser, Leander E. Keck, and Terence E. Fretheim. Nashville: Abingdon Press, 1994.

———. *Sabbath as Resistance: Saying No to the Culture of Now*. Louisville: Westminster John Knox Press, 2014.

Fretheim, Terence E. *Exodus. Interpretation: A Bible Commentary for Teaching and Preaching*. Louisville: Westminster John Knox Press, 1991.

Janzen, J. Gerald. *Exodus. Westminster Bible Companion*. Louisville: Westminster John Knox Press, 1997.

Wesley, John. *The Works of John Wesley*, vol. 3. Edited by Albert C. Outler. Nashville: Abingdon Press, 1986.

3. A SOOTHING, A STORY, AND A SONG

NUMBERS

MITCHEL MODINE

Introduction: A Staircase

Many Christians know the first two books of the Old Testament—Genesis and Exodus—far better than they know the next three—Leviticus, Numbers, and Deuteronomy. Part of the reason for this is the abundant legal material in these latter three books. While Exodus has some laws (most notably the Ten Commandments), it also contains a great deal of interesting stories. These stories have been told and retold and translated into many different kinds of media. To my knowledge, there has never been a children's story, or a novel for adults, or a popular movie made about the investigation by priests of various skin diseases (see Leviticus 13), or the extensive and repetitive offerings brought by leaders of the twelve tribes in dedication of the tabernacle (see Numbers 7), or the ritual of the firstfruits offering (Deuteronomy 26). No one expects all readers of the Bible to become familiar with these things, not to mention the hundreds more laws throughout the Bible's first five books. In fact, these books contain 613 different laws in all, and the interpretation of these laws runs to thousands and thousands of pages. However, willful ignorance of the Bible's legal material can lead—and has led throughout history—to some frightening and, frankly, evil conclusions. People have often said the Old Testament is a book of law while the New Testament is a book of grace. Moreover, people have said the Old Testament reveals a picture of a violent God while the New Testament reveals a picture of a loving God. These statements are not only inaccurate, but they were also condemned by the early church as heresy (false teaching).

A different understanding of one of the Bible's opening books—Numbers, in particular—is possible. While reaching a level of understanding of Jewish law similar to that of the rabbis is neither possible nor necessary for most people, it *is* both possible and necessary to have an encounter with the God of love when reading the legal material in the Old Testament. The book of Numbers is not well known among many Christian readers. Those with some biblical knowledge may know the famous priestly blessing from Numbers 6, which begins, "May the Lord bless you and keep you" (v. 24).[1] Others may know a little about the story of the non-Israelite prophet Balaam, particularly because of the interesting element of the prophet's talking donkey. I suspect only expert-level readers may recognize the name "Zelophehad" and know why the story of his daughters is important. However, when we read this book carefully, we can discover a lot of stories about the God of love. Legal material is legal material, but even here we can find some interesting things that may not have been expected.

I have been teaching the Bible at Asia-Pacific Nazarene Theological Seminary (APNTS) since 2008. My students have come from more than thirty nations and every inhabited continent. Even as an expert in the Old Testament, prior to living in the Philippines, I largely stayed away from the book of Numbers. I even found some old lecture notes recently in which I basically dismissed Numbers as unimportant, since it was only about—well, numbers. Indeed, the name of the book comes from the Greek translation of the Old Testament, the Septuagint. The title references the censuses that are taken in Numbers 1 and 26. By contrast, the Hebrew title is "In the Desert" (a single word in Hebrew). This title comes from a Hebrew word that appears in the first verse of the book. This word is the fifth word in the Hebrew text but the thirteenth word in the NIV.

In June 2012, I took a trip to the Malaysian countryside. While there, I attended, along with two others from APNTS, a conference of the Asia Theological Association (ATA). During a break, I went back to my room for something, and as I came out to the staircase, I met a gentleman from New Zealand named Dr. Bruce Nicholls, now retired from a long teaching and writing career. At that time, Dr. Nicholls served as the general publications editor for the ATA. One of the ATA's main publishing projects was a set of biblical commen-

1. All translations are the author's own unless otherwise noted.

taries written for pastors in the Asia-Pacific context. The *Asia Bible Commentary* (ABC) series seeks to provide commentary on the Bible with theological and pastoral concerns in the foreground. The commentaries are not overly technical like some others, and they focus on the concerns of local communities in Asia-Pacific.

When I met Dr. Nicholls, he invited me to contribute the *ABC* volume on Numbers. This volume had been assigned to my predecessor at APNTS, who had not been able to complete the assignment before he left the seminary and returned to pastoral ministry in South Korea. I remember clearly what Dr. Nicholls said to me at that time. In fact, when I introduced the published commentary six years later at the same meeting (this time in Manila), I recalled this statement to the general amusement of the audience. He said, "You have the task of making a boring book interesting." I accepted this challenge and set about my work. In the end, I can surely say that Numbers proved to be far more interesting and significant than I imagined.

A Soothing: The Priestly Blessing

Archaeology is the science dealing with learning about and describing ancient societies through the stuff they left behind. There is a popular misconception about archaeology that connects it to more conservative views of the Bible. This misconception suggests that archaeology can somehow prove the Bible to be historically and factually true. This theory received its fuel from several centuries' worth of attempts to prove this or that famous story and, thus, to prove everything the Bible says. Interestingly enough, many or most of the stories "biblical archaeologists" tried to prove true were from the Old Testament, even though the general view of church people toward the Old Testament was one of wanting to skip over the "boring books" to get to the more interesting New Testament—more interesting because it talked about Jesus.

Archaeology, however, can neither prove nor disprove the Bible. It cannot say, for example, whether God exists. It can merely demonstrate that a group of people lived and that they believed certain things about God and worshiped God in particular ways, through sacrifices of particular animals on an altar of a particular shape—or whatever. Archaeology as we know it today was created out of the scientific revolution, which was driven by the quest to go as far back in time as possible to show the historical origin of things and ideas. As far as proving the Bible goes, the best that archaeology can do is give a judgment of "plausible."

In 1979, archaeologists found two silver amulets while digging in an ancient gravesite near Jerusalem. Some years later, scholars determined that these amulets bore the so-called Priestly Blessing from Numbers 6:24–26. Though the letters were somewhat degraded after spending hundreds of years in the dirt, these amulets represent perhaps the oldest surviving texts from the Old Testament, dating from just before the Babylonian exile in the sixth century BCE. It is surely going too far to say that these amulets *prove* that God exists or that the Bible is historically accurate or that this part of the Bible is a factual record. But it appears that people believed the tradition of the blessing to be important enough to write it down on a couple pieces of silver, and then they or others thought it was useful to wear this blessing around their necks. In other words, people thought this text and the idea contained in it were important. So we can ask the questions: What did this text say that seemed so important? What do this text and its demonstrated importance for some people in the ancient world say to us about encountering the God of love?

The blessing itself is rather simple, but it is powerful. In the context of the story, God instructed Moses to command Aaron and his sons to bless the people using this formula. That the command went to Aaron and his sons established a principle that only a priest should be allowed to pronounce this blessing. This was one of the many rules associated with it. These rules were not meant to diminish the force of God's blessing but to enhance it. Many Christian traditions today, by analogy, make sure to note that a priest or other ordained minister should pronounce a blessing over the people as they depart worship. A blessing—or a benediction, to use an older word that comes from Latin and means "to speak well"—is much more than a prayer of dismissal.

In addition, we can learn a lot from the content of the blessing and the way it is expressed. In this passage, the Hebrew language uses a particular form of the verb that combines prediction, request, and permission. Also, the verbs have their object ("you") attached to them. Though the object of the verb is singular and masculine in every case, all worshipers are included as the object of God's blessing and concern. The priests giving this blessing are doing three things simultaneously. First, they are predicting that God will bless and keep the worshiper. (Important note: as with the objects of the verbs, all priests in ancient Israel were men, all descended from Aaron. Many churches have subsequently seen the Spirit of God at work in both men and women and have ordained them accordingly.) Second, they are requesting that God bless and keep the worshiper. This particular verb is sometimes used when an inferior-status person is demanding something of a superior-status person. Third, they are making space in the world for God's blessing and keeping to occur. In the beliefs of ancient Israel, speaking something had the effect of creating a world in which such a thing could be true. Incidentally, this is why telling the truth is so important; indeed, it is why telling the truth made it into the Ten Commandments. In a way, one creates worlds when one speaks.

What does this priestly blessing say about encountering the God of love? If the priests had said it on their own, there might remain a bit of uncertainty. If they simply predicted on their own initiative that God would bless God's people, the awful possibility that God would not do so would have still remained. Even though they endeavored to create a world in which God's blessing could flourish—and, for Jews, this was done by keeping God's law as God's people chosen for this purpose—they knew the possibility existed that other people would misunderstand their quest as mere legalism, ritualism, formalism, and other -isms. But this was not their own initiative. God commanded that the priests pronounce the blessing, thus committing to enact the blessing. Nevertheless, sometimes our lived experience attempts to belie this assurance. Wicked people continue to survive and thrive, sometimes even attacking the very people who are living out God's mission to repair the world through their adherence to God's law. For the people suffering as a result, the priests' prediction may indeed sound hollow. At the end of everything, however, the bells peal "more loud and deep" that "God is not dead, nor doth he sleep! The wrong shall fail, the right prevail, with peace on earth, good will to men!"—to use the words of one of my favorite Christmas hymns ("I Heard the Bells on Christmas Day," based on Henry Wadsworth Longfellow's 1863 poem "Christmas Bells").

In Numbers 6:24, the first verb, "bless," occurs at the very foundation of Israel as a people, from when God said that all the nations of the world would be blessed through God's blessing of Abraham (Genesis 12:1–2). The word "keep" draws the alert reader to Psalm 121, one of the best expressions in the entire Bible of God's watchfulness and care for God's people: God "will not allow your foot to stumble. The one who keeps you will not slumber. Hey! The keeper of Israel will neither slumber nor sleep" (vv. 3–4). As in Numbers 6, the verbs in Psalm 121 are singular, but these are not individualistic sayings. Ancient Israel—like almost all of its neighbor societies, both ancient and modern—was a communal society. This means the individual is always part of a community. God will not fall asleep on the job, either with you individually or with the entire community. In Numbers 6, the blessing also goes out to all of the children of Israel: "Thus they shall set my name upon the Israelites, and I will bless them" (v. 27).

In verse 25, the blessing calls for God's face to shine upon the people. Turning again to Psalms, one finds many prayers for God's face to shine upon God's people (4:6; 67:1; 80:3, 7, 19). In two instances, an individual asks for God's face to shine upon "me" or "your servant" (31:16; 119:135). When God's face shines upon someone, it means that God is gracious; the two ideas are not separate. One might say that God's face shining on someone *results* in God being gracious. This is a kind of royal image: when a king or queen looked with favor on one of their subjects, they were favorably inclined toward that person. If a royal face turned dark, the opposite was the case. But here, God's face is light! To dip into the New Testament a bit, 1 John 1:5 says, "God is light, and darkness is not in him at all."

Verse 26 picks up the same idea of God's face being friendly toward the worshiper. Here the phrase is "may God lift up God's face toward you." This may again reflect a royal context. Usually, when the king or queen came into a room, everyone bowed at least their heads, if not their entire bodies. Then the king or queen would often come and lift up the heads of those upon whom their favor rested at that moment. We can again look to the psalms to find some content like this. Psalm 27:6 says, "My head shall be lifted up above my enemies all around me." Sometimes enemies are not foreign adversaries but those who should be nearest and dearest. Yet, wherever enemies may be found, and even when it seems like only enemies are around, God is with God's people.

The image of God lifting up the worshiper's head is found again in Psalm 3: "O LORD, how many enemies do I have? How many people stand against me? Many people are talking about me [behind my back]. They say: 'There is no salvation for him in God.' But you, O God, are a shield behind me. You're my glory, and the one who lifts up my head" (vv. 1–3). When God lifts up the head and establishes peace for God's people (Numbers 6:26), even attacks from behind are thwarted. Even when one's closest friends have become enemies, God defends, shields, protects, and restores. At the end of the blessing, God's priests place God's name upon the Israelites, and God blesses them. What God says God will do, God will do.

A Story: Balaam's Donkey

The story of the non-Israelite prophet Balaam in Numbers 22–24 is famous because of the interesting element of the prophet's talking donkey. Many Christian readers of the Bible tend to skip over the Old Testament because of the apparent difficulty of its contents. As a result, many tend only to know the highlights, which unfortunately often leads to reducing the Old Testament to a series of moral lessons. These lessons take the character of persevering under suffering (Joseph, Job); being faithful to God in difficult times (Abraham, Ezra); achieving great things for God despite being considered inadequate (David, Esther); working hard to help people when others oppose you (Ruth, Nehemiah); and so on.

These stories about faithful humans are great, even though most of the better-known stories involve men as their central characters (see the next section). However, what if a reader were to consider the place of animals in the story? Maybe God loves animals as well as humans. A couple years ago, a student of mine was writing a thesis on the Day of Atonement (Leviticus 16). There is a particular part in this chapter in which the priest chose between two goats. One was sacrificed to God while the other was sent off to be eaten by a demon named Azazel. When we got tired after a long meeting, we got to wondering what, if anything, might be going through the goats' minds as this selection process was going on. Though these reflections may sound silly, the Old Testament does have at least one text speaking of God's concern toward animals. At the very end of the book of Jonah, in which God scolded the prophet for his narrow-mindedness, God asked, "Should I not be concerned about Nineveh, that great city, which has 120,000 inhabitants that do not know their right hand from their left, and also many animals?" (4:11).

Balaam was a famous figure in the ancient Near East. Archaeologists discovered an inscription in the Jordan River Valley that refers to Balaam, indicating his importance. Balaam is connected to three different deities in this text: Shgr, Ishtar, and Shadday. The deity

Shgr is unknown outside of this inscription. Ishtar is more famous as the consort of the god known as Marduk in the city of Babylon. Shadday may appear in the Bible, perhaps in the compound name El Shaddai, often translated as "God Almighty." God uses this name with Abraham in Genesis 17:1, among other places.

In the book of Numbers, King Balak of Moab hires Balaam the prophet to pronounce a curse upon the Israelites as they travel through the wilderness after leaving Egypt. Regardless of whether Balaam in the Bible is connected to Balaam in the inscription, the idea that a prophet-for-hire could be a powerful person makes a lot of sense. If Balaam were connected to many different deities, he probably had a reputation as an effective prophet whose word came true. Judging prophets by whether their words came true is an important idea that even appears in Deuteronomy 18:20–22. Balaam would not have passed the test in Deuteronomy, however, because he often spoke in the name of gods other than the LORD.

As the story goes, Balaam told King Balak that, payment or no payment, he would only be able to do what God told him to do (Numbers 22:18, 20). Nevertheless, in the course of time he seems to have become more stubborn. Balaam's stubbornness serves to introduce a very interesting part of the story. God used Balaam's donkey to communicate with the prophet. This is interesting not least because, earlier in the story, God interacted with Balaam directly (see 22:9–12). The donkey—the text makes clear that it was female—was able to see the angel of the LORD standing in the path. By contrast, Balaam, even though he was presented as a powerful, capable prophet, was not able to see the angel.

The donkey's role in the story is recounted in Numbers 22:21–35. Three times the donkey took steps to avoid the angel, perhaps out of fear. First she carried the prophet off the road and into a field. Balaam beat the donkey to force her back onto the road. The angel then appeared in the middle of a narrow pathway between two vineyards. The donkey, frightened again, tried to squeeze past the angel, whom only she could see. In the process, she ran Balaam into the retaining wall of one of the vineyards, hurting his foot. Balaam beat the donkey again. Then, for a third time, the angel appeared in the middle of a narrow road. Now the donkey had nowhere to go, so she simply lay down with Balaam still on her back. He became angry and beat her again.

At this point, the story takes a dramatic turn. In the first two instances, Balaam's stick was sufficient to get the donkey back on the desired path. This time, however, the donkey talked back to Balaam, wanting to know why he has mistreated her, when she has never disobeyed him in the past. Though the prophet wished he had a sword by which to kill the donkey, he admitted that, except for this time, she had always been a faithful animal. Suddenly he could see the angel, who talked to him just as the donkey did. The angel told Balaam that the donkey saved his life by disobeying.

Thus, the donkey played a critical role in the story. God ultimately wanted to frustrate King Balak's desire to have the Israelites cursed. Balaam was ultimately unable to utter any kind of condemnation; instead, he blessed the Israelites. Might one be able to say that the donkey was following the will of God? We cannot be sure, but if the angel had killed Balaam, Balaam would not have been able to deliver the blessing God desired. Moreover, the angel expressed concern for the donkey's well-being in Numbers 22:32–33. The donkey, the angel told Balaam, would have been spared while he himself would have been killed. The donkey saved his life—perhaps because God told her to do so, even if this entailed doing something she had never done: disobeying her master's direct commands.

A Song: Zelophehad's Daughters

Father Abraham had many sons
Many sons had father Abraham.
I am one of them, and so are you,
So let's just praise the Lord!"

Many people raised in the Protestant evangelical church—whether in the West or in places influenced by the West—are familiar with the children's song "Father Abraham." This song speaks to the continuity of God's care for God's people throughout history. However, over the last century or so, some readers of the Bible have grown uncomfortable with what appears to be an overemphasis on *men* and *men's* experience. In light of this, many scholars and leaders encourage church members, especially pastors and leaders, to be aware of and use gender-inclusive language. The biblical languages often use masculine terms to refer to all people, but that does not necessarily mean these languages sought to denigrate women. However, English usage has developed to the point that now it is problematic, and potentially harmful, to continue to follow this practice.

Encountering the God of love in the Old Testament requires witnessing and studying many different episodes, including those that defy our expectations. Paying close attention to the stories of women in the Bible can give believers a more complete picture of God's love active in the world. Numbers contains a story in which women appear powerful and confident, at least to a point. This is the story of the daughters of Zelophehad, a poor fellow who suffered the tragic fate of dying without sons in a patriarchal world. Zelophehad is mentioned twelve times in eight verses in the Old Testament, most of which are in Numbers 27 and 36. Numbers 26:33 sets the scene for the story of Zelophehad's daughters. The story that follows is in two parts—Numbers 27:1–11 and 36:1–12. The story is told again briefly in Joshua 17:3–4. Finally, 1 Chronicles 7:15 comments only that Zelophehad died without sons. Dying without sons created a problem in a patriarchal society because of the inheritance of property. In the words of his daughters, Zelophehad, who was a member of the exodus generation, "died for his own sin" (Numbers 27:3). The daughters did not specify what sin led to Zelophehad's death. They only made sure to point out that he did not participate in the rebellion of the Korahites, the story of which is related in Numbers 16.

Following the introduction of the daughters in 26:33, these daughters approached Moses in chapter 27 and laid out their case in an interesting fashion. Throughout the text, rather than arguing on their own behalf, they seemed to be concerned that their father's name not be lost to Israelite memory. The daughters spoke with one voice, which probably means that the oldest, Mahlah (named first in 26:33; 27:1; 36:11; and Joshua 17:3), spoke for all. Incidentally, Mahlah's name is similar to another man who died without children—Mahlon, the first husband of Ruth (Ruth 1:1–5). Their names mean "sick one" or "weak one," though Mahlah appears stronger than her later namesake, at least judging by her activity in this story. Some of the earliest examples of reading the Bible with women's experience in the foreground, in fact, took special note of the courage and strength of Zelophehad's daughters.

The daughters made their case that they should be able to inherit land since their father had no sons. Moses consulted with God, and God provided a legal remedy. In general, biblical laws are either simple ("do this; don't do that") or complex ("if this happens, do that."). God's speech to Moses here (Numbers 27:7–11) is an example of a complex law. The law God gave here seemed to anticipate all possible scenarios: a man's inheritance would belong to sons if there were any, to daughters if there were no sons, to brothers if no children at all, and to the nearest relative if there were no brothers. When we look at this from the perspective of God's love, we see God caring for those whom society might leave behind.

Some readers have wondered about the status of Zelophehad's wife. In fact, this point helps us recall the connection I suggested to Ruth above. In the book of Ruth, Naomi, having lost her husband and both her sons, set Ruth and Orpah free because she would not be able to provide more sons for them to marry. Orpah accepted her freedom, and Ruth did not. We do not know where Zelophehad's wife was. Since the text pays no attention to her, we might be able to assume she was also dead. Or, if she was alive, since the daughters had reached marriageable age—we know this from the second part of the story in Numbers 36:1–12—she may have been too old to attempt to bear any more children.

The societal situation suggested by this story is one where daughters could not inherit. It may have been the case that daughters were sometimes designated as heirs along with their brothers—or alone if they had no brothers—but God's response in Numbers 27 made it explicitly legal. When Moses talked to God, God expressed love and concern for the daughters. The daughters showed concern that their father's name not be blotted out of Israel's memory. God declared that they could inherit property so the daughters' names would not be forgotten either. This is an expression of the grace and love of God. Just as Abraham had many sons, so Zelophehad had only daughters. Just as the many sons of Abraham represented God's concern, so the daughters of Zelophehad represented God's concern. Girls join boys in singing, "Many sons had Father Abraham; I am one of them, and so are you." Could not, then, boys join girls in singing, "Only daughters had Zelophehad; I am one of them and so are you"?

Zelophehad's daughters also appear in Numbers 36. Unfortunately, this second episode almost reversed the gains made in chapter 27. To begin with, this chapter showed not the daughters coming forward but instead their male relatives. In addition, they came before "the heads of the Israelite families" (36:1) as opposed to "the whole assembly" (27:1). The biggest difference, however, comes in the content of the speech. We have already examined Numbers 27:3–4, so note here that, in 36:2–9, not only did the leaders express fear that their land should pass out of their clan if it were given to the daughters and they married, but Moses validated their fear, requiring the daughters to marry within their clan. He did this apparently without consulting God, even though the narrator insists that Moses spoke "according to the word of the LORD" (36:5).

Men's interests have reasserted themselves in Numbers 36, since the tribal leaders made something of an appeal based on the previous legal decision set down by Moses. They attempted to preserve the integrity of the inheritance within the clan by prohibiting Zelophehad's daughters from marrying outside the clan. Moreover, male members of the tribe expressed more concern for the land than for the daughters. Though the daughters had not placed *themselves* in greatest concern but their father instead, the tribal elders did not seem particularly concerned about Zelophehad at all.

In summary, chapter 27 seems more amenable to women's concerns, while chapter 36 seems more male-centered. The men stepped in to reassert the control they lost to the women who issued a challenge on behalf of their dead father. The daughters of Zelophehad constituted a special case in inheritance practices, mainly because they took the initiative to request a special dispensation from Moses and God. God granted their request because God's nature is love. God's love primarily reaches toward those who are less privileged in society.

Conclusion

When I met Dr. Nicholls on the staircase in the Malaysian countryside, he told me that Numbers was a boring book. As I wrote my commentary, I discovered that, in reality, it is far from boring. Though it is not well known, it contains much that can be important for Christians. In Numbers 6, God's blessing was assured, even in the face of overwhelming odds and opposition. In Numbers 22, God used a donkey to help bring about the conditions that allowed God's blessing to fall on the chosen people. Finally, in Numbers 27 and 36, God showed love and concern for those whom society may have forgotten.

Questions for Discussion

1. What do you think about the verbs in Numbers 6:24–26 (“bless,” “keep”)? How does God assure us of God’s blessing and concern?
2. What might the story of Balaam’s donkey tell us about how God cares about non-human elements of creation?
3. How can God use believers to care for those whom society may have forgotten? What are some key steps that can be taken to care for the disadvantaged?

4. ON LOVING THE GOD OF LOVE

DEUTERONOMY 6:4–5

MARTY ALAN MICHELSON

AMONG CHRISTIANS IN OUR TIME, John 3:16 is easily the most recognized and most memorized passage of Christian Scripture. Among persons of ancient Israelite faith, however, Deuteronomy 6:4–5 was likely the most recognized and most memorized passage of Hebrew Scripture.[1] Whereas John 3:16 is important and popular, Deuteronomy 6:4–5 has been important for centuries longer and popular for an entire millennium more. John 3:16 points with clarity to God's love for the world. Deuteronomy 6:4–5 also points to a God of love. And, while it is the case that all of Jesus's teaching is infused with theological ideas from the Scripture he studied, it is likely that Deuteronomy 6:4–5 is a passage Jesus recited daily—perhaps in the morning and in the evening, since this scripture calls hearers to remember and recite these words "when you lie down and when you rise" (v. 7, NRSV).

In addition to the likely reality that Jesus recited this passage about God's love daily, the idea of a loving God in Deuteronomy 6 informed specific events narrated to us in the Gospels. That means that Deuteronomy 6 not only formed the bookends of Jesus's days, but it also infused Jesus's way of being in the world. Deuteronomy 6, about a God of love, shaped how Jesus lived into and lived out the message of how this loving God calls for humans to love God and others. While every Gospel bears witness to the love of God made known in the life of Jesus, and while John's Gospel and letters uniquely highlight multiple features of God's love, it is in the Gospels of Matthew, Mark, and Luke where we read the evangelists' testimony that Jesus believed this passage from Deuteronomy to be central for discerning how to live as a believer. This passage from Deuteronomy was not simply central and important—it was a commandment that Jesus cited as the "greatest" and "first" commandment (Matthew 22:34–40).

---

1. For a full discussion of the passage under consideration in this article, see Marty Alan Michelson, *The Greatest Commandment: The LORD's Invitation to Love* (Oklahoma City: Dust Jacket Press, 2012).

The Call of a Loving God

Deuteronomy brings to culmination the first five books of the Bible. These first books serve as the foundation for discerning who God is in God's revelation. The first five books are known as the Torah, the Law, the Five Books of Moses, or the Pentateuch. Deuteronomy means "Second Law." The title derives from the fact that, in this book, Moses rephrases and restates the laws given at Sinai. The book is not a new law, a second edition, or a secondary law but the reiteration of the same core principles already established from Exodus 19 to Numbers 10, when the law was given at Sinai. The exact verses we explore have a special title associated with them. In Jewish tradition, Deuteronomy 6:4–9 is known by a title derived from the Hebrew word that begins the passage: the *Shema* ("Hear!").

Deuteronomy 6:4 (NRSV) opens, "Hear, O Israel: The LORD is our God, the LORD alone." Hearing is an important part of life. In traditional understandings in the Western world, hearing is considered to be one of five basic senses alongside sight, smell, touch, and taste. With these senses, we experience life, gain orientation, and relate to other things and persons. We hear sounds that make us smile—perhaps the giggle of a child. We hear sounds that motivate us to seek safety—perhaps the sound of a siren. In and through our hearing, we are able to stay in conversation and communication with people around us. Hearing is fundamental for our ability to live in conversation with others and in genuine relationship. Even when there is an impairment to the auditory nerve, we replace that sense with other forms of communication that allow for "hearing." In some key ways, being human is tied to our ability to hear because hearing is tied to our ability to communicate, and communication is at the core of what it means to be human since humans are relational beings.

So what does it mean to hear? We hear the TV playing in the other room; sometimes it is loud enough that we can discern what show is on or what team is playing which sport. Other times it is just a noise that we hear but cannot discern with great specificity. While sounds permeate our sensory experience all the time, we do not give attention to most of what we hear. In the midst of the sounds of life's daily existence, there are other sounds that compel our attention. Some sounds call for our response, like the ring of a phone, a knock on the door, or the voice of someone saying our name. These sounds, unlike the sound of rustling leaves or the appliance fan, call for us to hear them in a way that beckons something from us. Hearing, then, is not just a sense and sensation of many things all around us. It is an aspect by which we relate to the world and a means by which we enter into relationship.

The word "hear" as used in Deuteronomy 6:4 is about hearing beyond mere ambient noise around us. *Shema* in this verse means to hear the instruction of the LORD in order to understand God and God's relationship with human persons. Hearing God opens the possibility that we can enter into conversation and communication with God. The *Shema* invites people to give focus to the LORD by hearing. The LORD calls for hearing because the LORD wants to enter into relationship. While the most common translation for the Hebrew term at the start of verse 4 is "hear," this term involves more than hearing. The Hebrew word can also be translated as "listen." The nuance of listening is important because it requires something more from us. Listening requires more focus, in a particular way of tuning in and being aware and attentive. Listening is a deliberate mental attention. Sometimes when we are distracted from our listening, we say that we can't "hear," even though we *can* still hear—but our *listening* is impeded by competing noises and sounds. Listening is focused in specific ways with greater precision than hearing. In the best relationships, attentive and active listening is at the heart of clear, careful, focused conversation. When we have something important we want to communicate, we might request careful listening from our relational partners. We might lean into the ear of the one we love and, in the quietness of a whisper, call for their attuned awareness because we want them to listen carefully to, and discern correctly, our words of affection.

Deuteronomy 6:4–5 comes from the God of love, who calls to persons so they will hear *and* listen. Deuteronomy 6:4 is God's call for people to listen with intention and attention. There is, however, another aspect to the Hebrew term *Shema*. This term can also mean "obey." Obedience moves beyond hearing or listening, though it builds upon both. By doing actions that demonstrate obedience, a person proves that she or he has heard and listened. To obey is to respond with loyalty and deference to the words of the one who is communicating. I may have a sense that someone has heard me or listened to me, but I can only know for sure when their actions in response to my words become enacted and embodied. As a teacher in the classroom, I can explain assignments to students, provide information in lecture for students, give examples, and meet with students to ensure they *hear* how to do the work; yet I can only really know if what has been communicated is heard and listened to when learners bring their projects to me and demonstrate they have taken action. Actions show that the communication has been clear.

Obedience, then, is an embodied demonstration of the value we give to our relationships—whether in an organizational setting of hierarchy or in the mutuality of a relationship. When we love, trust, and respect others, we hear them, we listen to them, and we live a life that responds in shared obedience to what we have heard from them. *Shema*, the first word of God's invitation in Deuteronomy 6:4, beckons humans to respond relationally with hearing, listening, and obeying—all in one word.

The People Who Are Called

To take the next step of exploring the love of God expressed in the command of Deuteronomy 6:4–5, we can understand God's call here when we understand *who* is called into hearing, listening, and obedience. In 6:4, *Israel* is invited into relationship with God. When people in the twenty-first century read "Israel," they may rightly think of ancient Israelites. Yet the invitation is not limited to that one group but can also include us today, if we choose to respond to God's invitation.

When the Torah was given at Mount Sinai from God to Moses and the people who had come out of Egypt, the Israelites were not yet a nation. They had family connections and a tribal identity, though the Bible also tells us that Egyptians and a "mixed crowd" (Exodus 12:38, NRSV) came out of Egypt with the Hebrews to become part of God's people. Deuteronomy 6:4 was not initially addressed to an already existing nation. Rather, the call was made to a people who were on their way to becoming a nation. The verses that come before Deuteronomy 6:4 announce that this instruction is for "you and your children and your children's children" (v. 2, NRSV). The *Shema* was offered to a new generation who could take up the call to obey God's commands to become a holy nation and priestly kingdom (Exodus 19:1–6). This invitation becomes new in every new generation when new people live into it.

The *Shema* invites new persons in new generations to become a believing community alongside ancient believing communities. "O, Israel" can include any person who takes the time to hear, listen, and obey. When "O, Israel" is proclaimed, every new generation is called to live in accordance with the laws of God in the commandments. Every new generation is called to become God's people. We, today, can still receive and respond to God's call—along with persons of every nation, every language, every tribe, and every people—to partner with God in becoming a holy nation and priestly kingdom.

The God Who Calls

Deuteronomy 6:4 moves from "hear/listen/obey, O Israel" to a direct statement about God. God is a complex reality. The entire body of Scripture explains only a portion of who God is. For understanding the portrayal of God in Deuteronomy 6:4–5, we may look to the story of Moses and the burning bush in Exodus 3–4. There are many qualities and characteristics of God revealed in this famous passage, but certainly notable is the giving of God's personal name to Moses. God reveals to Moses that God's personal name is "YHWH" (see Exodus 3:14). This divine name (rendered "the LORD" in most English translations) reveals a personal, relational, loving God who makes God's own self available to Israel—and to every continuing present generation. The name means, "I am that I am" or "I will be who I will be" (Exodus 3:14).

Deuteronomy 6:4–5 uses this divine name to indicate the personal, present, and relational God who has a proximity of closeness and accessibility. The LORD demonstrates love by revealing personal access through a personal name. This personal God invites each present generation to respond. When strangers exchange names, they are no longer strangers. Likewise, when God gives God's name to humans, God makes God's self available to be called upon, to be known, and to be engaged in relationship. Our passage declares that the eternal, sovereign, sustaining, expansive, universal, cosmic God is "our God" (v. 4)—personal and intimate, close and proximate. The LORD, personally named, is *our* God, entering into relationship!

When Deuteronomy 6 declares that the LORD is our God, it is not claiming ownership of God in the same way that we claim ownership of property and possessions. Instead, it is like when we talk about "our" family. Family members are persons. We do not own them. We share relationships with them in reciprocal ways. This must be understood when we talk about "our God" made known at Sinai and then made known to all persons through the recorded words of Deuteronomy 6. God is not a thing for us to possess but one who exists in relationship with us. The LORD reveals the LORD's own self as a relational partner in a shared life as we hear, listen, and obey. The LORD as "our God" affirms a fundamental, complex truth about God: the LORD is relational. The LORD is known fundamentally and uniquely in relationship. The LORD as "our God" is relationally infinite, complex, wonderful, and worthy of praise.

The final words of Deuteronomy 6:4 (NRSV) are "the LORD alone." These words in Hebrew can also be rendered in English translation as "the LORD is one" and "the LORD our God is one LORD." The wording indicates that, although many persons share a relationship with the LORD, there are not separate lords or individual gods. The LORD our God, though existing in infinite relationships, is singular.

We have come to associate the name "YHWH" ("LORD") with the role of being sovereign over all things in heaven and on earth and under the earth. But this name is not a mere title. Let me offer an analogy. I carry multiple titles or roles in life. In church settings, people most often refer to me as Pastor Marty. At the university where I teach, I am rarely called Pastor Marty and instead might be addressed as Dr. Michelson—a different title and a different part of my name. I have also had nicknames at various times. The teacher of my middle-school woodshop class many years ago called me Martha—not my name or gender, yet in middle school, from this teacher, I answered to it. While I may answer to other nicknames from a few friends or use a particular title in some professional settings, anyone who genuinely knows me knows that my real name is Marty (and not Martin!). The essence of my oneness—if I can say it like that—is that I am, singularly, the one entity identified in space and time as Marty Alan Michelson.

Theologians and scholars have nuanced the essence of the LORD's oneness—a unified whole. Theologians and scholars have nuanced the aloneness of God as the only God—monotheism. Theologians and scholars have nuanced the oneness of God as relationally complex—Trinity. Yet, perhaps in Deuteronomy 6:4–5, this "alone" or "one" nature of God really means to emphasize the utterly personal, approachable, relational "One" who invites us to hear, listen, and obey. The LORD is "our God"—no other titles necessary. This is our

God "alone," and this one God has been made available to us. The LORD is one, even if we are many in relationship to this one. This is a singular God who invites any who would choose to hear, listen, and obey.

The Demands of the Call

Deuteronomy 6:5 (NRSV) addresses those who would respond to God: "You shall love the LORD your God with all your heart, and with all your soul, and with all your might." In verse 4, the one God in relationship with persons called for hearing, listening, and obedience. The key issue involved in encountering this loving God is now made known in what this God commands. What are the demands this God will give? What will be required in the obedient submission of human persons? The LORD could demand anything! What will it be?

Here are the words: "You shall love." The command of the *Shema* is not to a number of "do this" and "don't do this" lists. The command is a single, simple verb—love! We are to love. We are to *be* loving. We are to be lov*able*. We are to partner in relational love. We are to participate in relationships with the LORD, motivated by love. We are to generate relationships of love, to exist in love, and to extend love. Love is what the LORD wants us to hear. Love is what the LORD calls us to discern as we listen. Love is what the LORD calls us to obey. The LORD, who alone is our God, does not come to manipulate humans, nor is the intent of God to require harsh impositions that restrict life. The LORD comes fundamentally and specifically to invite a diverse family of many to become a community of generous, relational grace in the context of love.

The command in Deuteronomy 6:4–5 is from a generously relational, life-giving God who calls for reciprocity and relationship, wholeness and health, in love. The God of love revealed in Deuteronomy is a present, existing, aware God who lives in relationship to all persons as "our God." This is a God who wants, more than anything else, a people of loving obedience who are invited to partner with God in mutual love.

Deuteronomy 6:5 (NRSV), after announcing God's call "you shall love," goes on to say, "You shall love the LORD your God with all your heart, and with all your soul, and with all your might." The Hebrew words used here are *leb* ("heart"), *nephesh* ("soul"), and *meod* ("might"). None of these words is uncommon in the Old Testament, and they can all be translated in more than one way. Each has important layers of meaning, and the last word, *meod*, I find to be particularly exciting for reflection upon the God of love and the divine call on God's people.

Twice in the Gospels, in Mark 12:3 and Matthew 22:37, Jesus used Deuteronomy 6 as the basis for answering questions from others about the first or greatest commandment. A third occurrence of this passage appears in Luke 10:27, not in the words of Jesus but in the words of a lawyer who questions Jesus about what he must do to inherit eternal life. Mark and Luke say we should love the LORD our God with our heart, soul, mind, and strength. Matthew says we should love the LORD our God with our heart, soul, and mind. In Deuteronomy 6:5, no term for "mind" is explicitly present, but it uses the word "heart" (*leb*), which in the Old Testament can include the meaning of "mind." The Hebrew word for "heart" is not primarily about knowledge, the brain, or the IQ. When Deuteronomy 6:5 says we are to love God, there is no obligatory or expected sense that loving God involves brain power or having correct ideas about God. In the Greek context of the Gospels, however, with the rise of philosophy and education, correct thinking and right ways of discerning content were important. It is possible that the Gospels use "heart and mind" as a means to translate the complex notion of *leb* from Hebrew into their changed context.

Today the world values high education and correct thinking. Education is seen as crucial and central to our existence. Most areas have compulsory education that seeks to ensure that children grow up learning the "right answers" to the "right questions" about various subjects. We teach for correct thinking, and we measure people's aptitude based on test scores and GPAs. But Deuteronomy 6:5 requires no test to determine whether one has the right knowledge about the LORD before they are called to love the LORD. Deuteronomy 6 beckons persons to love, and anyone is capable of responding.

In fact, in the Old Testament, the Hebrew term for "heart" carries the meaning of the inward person, mind, or will. The full complexity of the word should not be oversimplified, yet it might be worth noting that the first appearances of the word in the Old Testament are in Genesis 6:5–6, where the same word is used to describe the intention of humans (evil) and the pathos of God (grief). "Heart" in the Old Testament is about intention and emotion more than mind and cognition. The nuance is important for Deuteronomy 6:4–5. Here we are called to love the LORD our God with all of our *leb*. This means we love God with something like the sum total of our heart-emotions-mind. This kind of loving is not about having right answers or right thoughts as much as it is about having an appetite that craves this love. What is certain is that, in loving the LORD our God with our "heart," we are not giving mental and cognitive agreement to a logical belief; instead, we are extending our intention and desires in love.

The second word used to describe how God's people should love is *nephesh*. This Hebrew term can be translated numerous ways, including "soul, living being, life, self, person, desire, appetite, emotion, and passion." The best way to get a sense of this word is to go back to the first time it appears in the Old Testament. *Nephesh* is first used of animals or creatures that are living beings. In Genesis 1:20, 21, and 24, *nephesh* is used to describe the swarming creatures in the skies and in water and on land. The term is used of humans for the first time when God breathes the breath of life and the human becomes a living being (*nephesh*) in Genesis 2:7. *Nephesh*, then, means something about being animate and animated—being alive and existing. The idea of "soul" tries to capture this, but "soul" alone does not capture the full meaning, which includes "animation, alive, and existence." To love the LORD our God with all our *nephesh* means to love God with all of our existence and animation.

The third key Hebrew word Deuteronomy 6:5 is *meod*, often translated as "strength" or "might." We miss something, however, when *meod* is translated in these ways. The term *meod* is not a noun in Hebrew, nor an adjective; it is an adverb. That means this word is shaping the verb, not the noun. The word can be translated in many ways, including forcefully or exceedingly. Used in Deuteronomy 6:5, *meod* means that we are to love exceedingly and forcefully. Our love is to be characterized by extremeness and abundance—a "muchness" or a might. We could say that it is meant to be an extreme love.

Conclusion

Deuteronomy 6:4–5 calls us to love God with all of our emotion, volition, and intent. To love the LORD our God with all our *nephesh* means to love God with all of our existence and animation. And the term *meod* means that we love exceedingly and extremely. Perhaps an alternate translation for this verse could be that we are invited to "love exceedingly the LORD with the sum total of our intentional and emotional being." The God of love calls God's people to love, and this is truly inclusive and open for all. A person's age, aptitude, and abilities do not negatively impact the opportunity to love God. Understood in this way, the love that the LORD calls for is not about a disproportionate quality or quantity of love from anyone. Rather, love emerges from an equal effort from any person—whoever they are and however they are constituted—as they love the LORD with all that they are, with the fullness of their being directed to the LORD. The loving God of Scripture does not discriminate! The LORD does not exclude anyone from being able to live in relationship with God. Deuteronomy 6:4–5 calls us to orient our lives to God and God's love as those who love the LORD our God.

Questions for Discussion

1. How have you previously understood what it means to love God? How does Deuteronomy 6:4–5 add to your understanding of this call on our lives?
2. If we are to love God, then we are also to love others (see Matthew 22:34–40). What things sometimes hinder you from showing wholehearted, genuine love toward others, and how does Deuteronomy 6:4–5 encourage you to overcome those obstacles?
3. What are some practical ways that you can love God with all your heart in the activities of your daily life?

Bibliography

Michelson, Marty Alan. *The Greatest Commandment: The LORD's Invitation to Love.* Oklahoma City: Dust Jacket Press, 2012.

5. THE FAITHFUL LOVE OF GOD

RUTH 2:1–23

JENNIFER M. MATHENY

"Go back?" he thought. "No good at all! Go sideways? Impossible! Go forward? Only thing to do! On we go!" So up he got, and trotted along with his little sword held in front of him and one hand feeling the wall, and his heart all of a patter and a pitter."[1]

IN CHAPTER 5 of J. R. R. Tolkien's *The Hobbit,* Bilbo Baggins is frightened and alone, wondering what his next move will be in this dark and lonely place. With limited options, he resolves to move forward as he tells himself, "On we go!" Similarly, after a season of immense loss, Ruth decides there is no going back to Moab. Ruth demonstrates a resolve that resonates deep and bubbles up and out in the form of an oath commitment to her mother-in-law, Naomi. She commits to life with Naomi, venturing to Bethlehem, into an unknown place and with the sting of death at her heels.

The book of Ruth invites the reader to come along on this journey into the unknown. Themes of famine and harvest, emptiness and fullness, death and life, hidden and seen entice the reader to lean in and listen. This seemingly simple yet theologically rich story pulls the reader in with ponderings of divine presence and absence, ambiguity, and human agency. The God of love is revealed in Ruth's story, particularly in chapter 2, where we witness the love of God through human speech and actions in deeply profound moments. Specifically, God's faithful love takes the form of the sacrificial and generous actions of the characters in the story. Ruth 2:1–23 is a primary example of how the love of God is made known through particular people in Ruth's story. As the story progresses, it becomes clear that, even though God's presence may not be perceived as easily in the story of Ruth as in other Old Testament stories, the book of Ruth reveals the hidden presence of God through the speech and actions of Ruth and Boaz.

---

1. J. R. R. Tolkien, *The Hobbit, or There and Back Again* (New York: Random House, 1982), 69.

The Place of Ruth in Scripture

The story of Ruth takes place "in the days the judges were judging" (Ruth 1:1).[2] In the Christian canon, Ruth appears between Judges and 1 Samuel. The political transition between the era of judges into the monarchy in Israel is interrupted by this intimate story of a family—in particular, the plight of three widows. This story closely follows the lives of these women in a season of grief and loss. Naomi expressed her pain by renaming herself Mara, meaning "bitter" (1:20). The dark ending of the days of the judges—with death through tribal warfare and the kidnapping of women (Judges 19–21)—had not wholly subsided, though it cast a different shadow of death over these women.

Ruth is one of only two books in the Old Testament named after a woman (see also Esther). One of the central features unique to the Ruth story is that Ruth is a Moabite. It is unusual to have a story within the traditions of Israel about a Moabite woman. Looking back at the calling of Abraham in Genesis 12:1–3, the people of God were called to be a blessing to all nations. This call of blessing and inclusion reveals itself through this one intimate story that features famine-affected widows arriving in an Israelite village. The loving call of God, beginning with Abraham, to both receive and extend the blessing of God, formed a holy and missional people. The history of this people is gathered in the stories of scripture, and we discover this blessing in unexpected ways in the story of Ruth, as well as in our own lives and the communities in which we live.

The Genre of Ruth

The question of the book of Ruth's genre has been a vital part of the discussion of Ruth's purpose and function in the Old Testament. Proposals have identified the book of Ruth as similar to everything from a charming and idyllic story or a nursery tale to a historical

2. Biblical translations are those of the author, unless otherwise noted.

narrative. But the genre of a text also encompasses its shared social location, intended function, and rhetorical aim. Ruth ends with a genealogy that connects to the future Israelite monarchy by giving the lineage of King David (4:18–22).

Many scholars identify Ruth as a short story. Perhaps it is better, however, to see the book of Ruth as a type of literature referred to in the Old Testament by the Hebrew word *mashal*. This term refers to a kind of instructional literature like a proverb or parable but can also include prophecies, discourses, riddles, and even historical memoirs.[3] Ruth seems to be a *mashal* that communicates to and instructs its readers particularly through the use of dialogue among the characters in the story (we might even call the story of Ruth a dialogue-based *mashal*).

So what is the *mashal* of Ruth trying to teach its readers? Ruth's date of composition is difficult to determine, and different proposals entail various possibilities for why the story was important to a particular community in a specific historical context. Whatever its precise origins, the story of Ruth tries to instruct readers in any setting that God's purposes are continually being worked out through the chosen and holy people, often in surprising and obscure places. These holy people are called to love God and to love one another (Deuteronomy 6:4–5) and to be a blessing to the entire world (Genesis 12:1–9). Hence, Ruth is, in some ways, a timeless teaching (*mashal*) for the people of God. Ruth contributes to a robust conversation in the Old Testament that wrestles with critical theological, political, social, and personal questions.

The Theology of Ruth

It is often difficult to see the love of God through tragic stories, especially when God is not mentioned very often, divine appearances are absent, and prayers are limited. The book of Ruth has often been

3. See Kandy Queen-Sutherland, *Ruth and Esther, Smyth and Helwys Bible Commentary* (Macon, GA: Smyth and Helwys, 2016).

neglected in comprehensive treatments of Old Testament theologies for this very reason. At first glance, God seems absent in Ruth, and there are notable moments of ambiguity. How is one to discern the activity of God in stories of perceived divine absence? Can the love of God be found in these types of accounts?

Ruth is a story that reveals the love of God through human actions—or, put another way, through human *agency*. Prior to our focus text in Ruth 2, an early moment in the book shows this overall theology. In Ruth 1, Naomi urged her newly widowed daughters-in-law, Orpah and Ruth, to return to their homes in Moab. Naomi hoped they would be able to secure a future for themselves with new husbands. Orpah followed Naomi's suggestion, but Ruth chose to remain with Naomi, to journey this season with Naomi, even to death. Ruth made an oath of commitment: "Then Ruth said, 'Do not plead with me to leave you and return after you. For wherever you go, I will go; wherever you live, I will live; your people will be my people and your God my God. Wherever you die I will die, and there I will be buried. This may the Lord do to me and this he will add to, if even death will divide us'" (vv. 16–18).

This oath is unique in the Old Testament for several reasons. Ruth's statement does not contain the two Hebrew nouns normally associated with the idea of an oath, but she does use an oath formula ("this do . . . then this do again") that appears in several places throughout the books of 1 and 2 Samuel and 1 and 2 Kings. When an oath in this form appeared elsewhere in the Old Testament, it was spoken by a man in a commanding position. Here, the woman Ruth powerfully asserted her agency to proclaim how she would be faithful to Naomi even to death. The oath most closely associated with Ruth's is found in 1 Samuel 20:12–15. In a similar way to how Ruth risked her future in Moab to journey back with Naomi to Israel, so Jonathan forfeited his right to the throne, proclaiming allegiance to David. The seriousness of these oaths in the Old Testament is demonstrated through the invocation of God's name. The oaths by Ruth and Jonathan are the only oaths in the Old Testament that invoked the name of YHWH—Israel's covenant God.

In 1 Samuel 20:12–15, Jonathan proclaimed an oath of faithfulness to David and asked David to show him the love of the Lord. The verb translated "to show" is one of activity that far exceeds a verbal acknowledgment. The same Hebrew verb could also mean "to do" or "to make." The kind of love Jonathan requested was one that expresses itself through the heart, words, and hands. This love is sacrificial, lifts up the other, and places the other before oneself. The Hebrew term used for the kind of love represented by Jonathan's oath is *hesed* (see 1 Samuel 20:14–15). The term is translated as "faithful love" (NRSV); "steadfast love" (ESV); "lovingkindness" (NASB1995); "unfailing kindness" and "kindness" (NIV). The term is difficult to define. In context, however, it designates a kind of covenantal/relational love that reflects God's character but is often revealed through human actions toward others. It is a term encompassing salvation, preservation of life, the love of humanity toward God and toward one another. It is the covenant loving-kindness of God's faithfulness to us, often lived out in extravagant ways, usually within humanly impossible situations. The term appears in the Old Testament as something higher than the heavens and enduring forever (Psalms 36:5; 136); as part of a victory song by Miriam, proclaiming the love of God through saving acts (Exodus 15:13); as a type of care for the needy and lowly (Proverbs 3:3; 19:22); and as better than sacrifice and worth cultivating (Hosea 6:6; 10:12). It is love performed, lived out through human expressions within Israel's history.

The term *hesed* does not appear in Ruth's oath in chapter 1, but it occurs at other key places in the book (1:8, 20; 3:10). Moreover, it represents the way we see God's love in the actions and relationships of the human characters in Ruth.

God's Faithful Love Revealed in Ruth

God's *hesed* ("faithful love") is shown in Ruth specifically when it permeates the self–sacrificing actions of Ruth and Boaz to care for others in practical ways. This is a love story that involves risk to estate, reputation, and future. The faithful love of God manifests itself through the lives within the small community in Bethlehem, revealing the generous heart of God. One of the foremost ways that the faithful love of God is revealed in Ruth is through the encounters between people. Seen in this way, God is not absent in the book of Ruth but is operating profoundly and lovingly through human agents.

The Backstory to Ruth 2

Ruth 1 provides the backstory of these widows and the fears they carried into chapter 2. The motif of seed (produce and progeny) moves this story along even from the opening verses. A famine in Israel was the reason Elimelech and Naomi became displaced initially and migrated to Moab. Elimelech and Naomi made this journey with their two sons, Mahlon and Chilion. Sometime after reaching Moab, Elimelech died (1:3). Naomi's two sons married Moabite women, Orpah and Ruth, and at this point had been living in Moab for a decade (1:5). Suddenly and without any reason given by the narrator, Mahlon and Chilion died too. The names of these men alert Hebrew readers that their deaths were not completely unexpected. Mahlon's name means "sickly," and Chilion's name means "weakling," or "annihilation."

Three widows now take center stage in the story. Naomi decided to migrate back to Bethlehem (literally, "the house of bread") because the famine had subsided (v. 6). Naomi urged her daughters-in-law, Orpah and Ruth, to stay home in Moab and build new lives (v. 9). Naomi believed remarrying would give the two widows the security they needed. The young widows wept and initially told her, "No, we will return with you to your people" (v. 10). But Naomi insisted, stating that she was too advanced in years to bear more sons and that her situation was far worse than theirs. Naomi lamented that the hand of the LORD was against her (v. 13). She does not pray directly to God in this story but speaks about God's activity in her life as she perceives it.

Orpah eventually did what Naomi urged. But Ruth clung to Naomi and made the covenant oath we have already noted (vv. 16–17). Naomi silently relented, and there is no more recorded speaking on the journey to Bethlehem. They returned at the beginning of the barley harvest (v. 22).

Once they arrived, the women of the town asked, "Is this Naomi?"

Naomi responded out of her grief: "Do not call me Naomi. Call me Mara, for El Shaddai has dealt bitterly with me. I went away full, but YHWH has brought me back empty" (v. 21). Naomi continued speaking bitterly, accusing the LORD of causing evil in her life (vv. 20–21). Strangely, she did not mention Ruth, the young woman who pledged life and loyalty to her. Naomi declared her life empty as Ruth silently stood nearby.

God's Faithful Love Revealed by Ruth to Naomi (Ruth 2:1-7)

The opening scene in chapter 2 relays the information to the reader that Naomi had a family member ("kinsman") on her deceased husband's side, and his name was Boaz (v. 1). At this point in the story, the reader is given this bit of information in anticipation of God's provision. This opening line alerts the reader to this new character, though he is veiled at this point from Naomi and Ruth. After her oath in chapter 1, Ruth was silent until this moment. Naomi did not speak to or about Ruth after the oath. Ruth took the initiative and asked Naomi, "Please let me go to the field and glean . . . after one in whose eyes I find grace" (v. 2).

The opportunity for the poor and foreigners to glean was mandated by the law in Leviticus 19:9–10: "Now when you reap the harvest of your land, you shall not reap to the very edges of your field, nor shall you gather the gleanings of your harvest. And you shall not glean your vineyard, nor shall you gather the fallen grapes of your vineyard; you shall leave them for the needy and for the stranger. I am the LORD your God" (NASB; see also Leviticus 23:22; Deuteronomy 24:19).

Ruth's phrase "in whose eyes I find grace" refers to seeking the favor of someone in a dominant position. A notable example is when Joseph was placed second in command over Egypt, and the Egyptians sought his aid, asking, "Let us find grace/favor in your eyes" (Genesis 47:25). Ruth was aware that she would be in a vulnerable position as a gleaner, as a woman, and as a Moabite (a foreigner). Naomi responded, "Go, my daughter" (Ruth 2:2). One cannot help but wonder if some further instruction should have been given to Ruth. This was Naomi's hometown. She knew the fields; she knew the people; she probably knew the local gossip. Ruth would be vulnerable in the fields; nevertheless, she persisted, eager to take care of her mother-in-law.

As Ruth entered the field to glean, the text uses the phrase "as it happened" or "she chanced upon" to describe how she ended up in Boaz's field (v. 3). The Hebrew terms communicate a sense of fate, or chance. The only other place this particular phrase is found is Ecclesiastes 2:14, where God's presence appeared even more distant.[4] This phrase relays the idea that Ruth had no idea whose field she entered for gleaning. This portrayal highlights the notion of the surprise of God's presence that can appear absent to a person until retrospective insight is given.

The first words from the lips of Boaz were words of blessing to the reapers: "The LORD be with you!" (Ruth 2:4). Boaz was not only a wealthy kinsman and owner of the field; he was also a godly man. The reapers responded by blessing Boaz in return (v. 4). Turning to the foreperson, Boaz inquired about Ruth. He was aware of all who

---

4. For a detailed comparative study of Ruth 2:3 and Ecclesiastes 2:14, see Brittany Melton, *Where Is God in the Megilloth? A Dialogue on the Ambiguity of Divine Presence and Absence* (Leiden, Netherlands: Brill, 2018), 136–63.

were in his fields. Boaz inquired, "Who is this young woman?" (v. 5). Belonging and identity are wrapped up in this question.

The servant answered, "It is a young Moabite woman. She is the one who returned with Naomi from the land of Moab" (v. 6). It was clear from the foreperson's report that Ruth had been working tirelessly. He relayed to Boaz that she had asked, "'Please let me glean and gather the sheaves after the harvesters.' Now she had come in and she stood at that time of the morning until now. She has only been sitting at the house for a little while" (v. 7).

Ruth's ethnicity permeates the story. This foreperson stated that Ruth was a Moabite, Boaz would mention her ethnicity twice (4:5, 10), and the narrator alerts readers to her foreignness four times (1:4, 22; 2:2, 21). Genesis 19 gives a negative portrayal of the origins of the Moabites and Ammonites in the incestuous tale of Lot's daughters. Throughout the Old Testament, the Israelites and Moabites have a contentious relationship. Deuteronomy 23:4–7 forbids Moabites from assembly with Israel. But the enmity between these two people groups deconstructs slightly in the opening chapter of Ruth. Naomi's family fled to Moab during the famine as a place to survive. Rather than hostility, Naomi's family seems to have been received with hospitality, residing there for ten years. Though these two peoples were at odds in many instances, primarily due to their worship of different gods, they were geographical neighbors and shared a common ancestry (through Abraham and Lot). The relationship between the Israelites and Moabites was more complicated than it seems on the surface.

God's Faithful Love Revealed by Boaz to Ruth (Ruth 2:8–16)

Foreign identity is critical within this story as it plays out with Ruth's Moabite identity. It is clear that her otherness played a significant role in her vulnerability and heightened the opportunity for violence in the open field. Boaz saw this and quickly took charge. He instructed Ruth to remain in his field, to stay close to the other young women (Ruth 2:8). He also added, within earshot of the foreperson and other servants, "Have I not commanded the young men not to touch you? When you are thirsty, go to the vessels and drink from that which the young men have drawn" (v. 9). It is clear from this command that Ruth could be in danger of sexual abuse and other forms of violence in the fields. Boaz offered provision and protection in this critical moment—in this field upon which Ruth has supposedly "chanced."

The next scene features a dialogue about identity. As a Moabite immigrant gleaner, as a woman, and as a widow, Ruth expected to remain invisible. She was among the marginalized in this place. After Boaz spoke to her, Ruth fell on her face and bowed low to the ground. This bow indicates a bit of shock on Ruth's part. She responded with a wordplay: "For what reason have I found grace in your eyes that you *noticed* me, since I am a *foreigner*?" (v. 10). Here, "noticed" (*nakar*) and "foreigner" (*nokhri*) form an auditory play on words in Hebrew. Listeners to the story would pick up on this literary artistry. Ruth was genuinely shocked to be noticed, especially as a Moabite woman.

In the next part of the conversation, Boaz informed Ruth that he had been filled in about who she was. He said, "I have been told all that you have done for your husband's mother after the death of your husband, how you left your father, your mother, and the land of your birth and went to a people who you did not know previously. May YHWH reward your work and may your wages become complete from YHWH, the God of Israel, under whose wings you have come to seek refuge" (vv. 11–12). The reader is not privy to how Boaz gained all this information, but it is clear that he was a man who was in the know. Perhaps Boaz learned about this young Moabite woman in conversations around town, now that Naomi had returned. In this moment, perhaps he connected the dots. Boaz recognized Ruth's devotion to Naomi. He acknowledged all she had left ("the land of your birth") to go to a foreign people. This wording should remind readers of the call of Abraham in Genesis 12:1–3 to leave his homeland. Ruth's devotion to Naomi was recognized by Boaz as an act of faithfulness—an act of *hesed*—one that was reminiscent of the faith of Abraham.

Ruth responded to Boaz in a way similar to the oath she proclaimed in chapter 1: "Let me find grace in your eyes, my lord, because you have comforted me when you have spoken to the heart of your servant, although I am not as one of your servants" (Ruth 2:13). Boaz showed Ruth the "faithful love" of God through his words, and Ruth said, "you have comforted me." The word used for "comfort" is one that "appears in the Bible after major crises," such as the traumatic experience of exile (see Isaiah 40:1–2).[5] Additionally, the idiom "speak to the heart" is found in only nine places in the Old Testament (Genesis 34:13; 50:21; Judges 19:3; Ruth 2:13; 2 Samuel 19:7; 2 Chronicles 30:22; 32:6–7; Isaiah 40:2; Hosea 2:16). Ruth is the only woman to use this phrase, and she is a Moabite! Most uses of this idiom are spoken by men in powerful positions—kings and other political leaders, or prophets. Here again, Ruth is full of surprises and charts a path of agency in critical moments. Ruth navigated her identity in this short conversation with Boaz. From an initial sense of invisibility as a Moabite foreigner (Ruth 2:10), she later designated herself as "servant" (v. 13). This term carried the implication of a female slave, perhaps indicating that she recognized her lower status and that it made her ineligible for marriage. Eventually, this shift in identity would be noted by Boaz, when he verbally elevated her identity to that of a "woman of valor" (*eshet hayil*) in 3:11. After that she would become the "wife" of Boaz, elevating her identity even further (4:13). Ruth was seen by Boaz, through his eyes of grace, as a woman who sacrificed her home of Moab and journeyed in faith to an unknown land and an unknown people.

Later that day, at mealtime, Boaz invited Ruth to eat with the reapers (2:14), and thus to be part of this new community. Boaz ex-

---

5. Tamara Cohn Eskenazi and Tikva Frymer-Kensky, *Ruth: The JPS Bible Commentary* (Philadelphia: The Jewish Publication Society, 2011), 39.

tended a hand of hospitality, handing Ruth roasted grain. She ate until she was full (there were even leftovers) (v. 14). The idea of abundance, alongside the motifs of famine and harvest and empty and full, is prominent in this scene. In particular, this motif of leftovers from eating appears in 2 Kings 4:43–44 and 2 Chronicles 31:10, both of which illustrate the abundant provision of God.

After Ruth ate, she returned to the field to continue gleaning. Once again, Boaz took a protective stance toward Ruth. Boaz commanded the servants, “Let her gather between the sheaves and do not humiliate her. And also, pull out for her from the bundles of grain and leave them for her to gather, and do not rebuke her” (Ruth 2:15–16). Boaz was aware of what could happen to Ruth in the field, and he commanded them not only to hold back their harsh rebukes but also to show her extravagant kindness. He told them to pull out bundles of grain for her to gather—which was an incredible act of generosity that went above and beyond the law. Boaz revealed the faithful love of God through provision, protection, and comfort to this young Moabite widow.

God’s Faithful Love Revealed by Boaz to Naomi, Ruth, and the Deceased Husbands (Ruth 2:17–23)

After gleaning in the field until evening, Ruth beat out what she had gathered, and it amounted to around an ephah of barley (2:17). This work entailed separating the grain from the husks. For transport, the grain was most likely wrapped up in her apron, bulging greatly as she carried it home to Naomi. The ephah probably equaled almost thirty pounds of grain! One day’s typical gathering would have been more like two pounds.

When Ruth returned home, Naomi was astonished at all the grain Ruth held. Naomi asked where Ruth gleaned and proclaimed a blessing upon the one in whose field Ruth gathered (v. 19). Ruth informed Naomi that she had been working in the field of a man named Boaz (. 19). Naomi spoke of the *hesed* of God in this moment as she exclaimed, “May he be blessed of YHWH, who has not withheld his *hesed* from the living and the dead" (v. 20). Here, Naomi witnessed the faithful love of God through Boaz. More literally, Naomi said, "God has not abandoned his *hesed.*" Naomi's earlier description of herself as bitter entailed feelings of abandonment. Ruth brought proof, bulging through her apron, that God had seen them and not forgotten them.

Through the performative nature of love lived out in the lives of those around her, Ruth found grace in someone's eyes and was comforted (2:2), and Naomi's perception of God shifted. Though Naomi does not pray directly to God in this story, she attested to God's presence through her words to others (e.g., to Orpah and Ruth in 1:9; to the women of Bethlehem in 1:20–21; to Ruth in 2:20).

Naomi recognized the name Boaz. He was a relative, and also what is known in Hebrew as a *go'el*, a family redeemer. How Boaz will redeem will be discovered in the next two chapters. Ruth will request that Boaz enact a marriage (see Deuteronomy 25:5–10). Boaz was not obligated to perform this duty under the law. In fact, there was a closer redeemer who could fulfill this role (3:12). This nameless redeemer dismissed the opportunity as too costly, and in the end, Boaz provided for the impoverished family as an act of faithful love. The bulging apron of seed was symbolic of the life that was to come. Not only would the dead be remembered (2:20), but the name of the dead would also eventually be raised back to life at the close of the story (4:10).

Conclusion

Discovering the faithful love of God in Ruth is not a simple task and requires reflection beyond an initial reading. Ambiguity, perceived divine absence, and human agency are intentional elements of the Ruth story. But the *hesed* of God is revealed through the actions of human beings, such as Ruth's passionate oath and faithfulness to Naomi (1:16–18), Ruth's provision for Naomi (2:2–16), and the generosity of Boaz through kindness, protection, and provision (2:5–23).

For many, this sense of a perceived divine absence hits home in our own experiences during seasons of grief, loss, and transition. Even at the close of the Ruth story, many questions remain. In the final chapter, however, the women of Bethlehem praised Ruth as one in the line of the great matriarchs of Israel: Rachel, Leah, and Tamar. Ruth was praised as a woman who was "better than seven sons" (4:15). Initially identified as a Moabite outsider, the story comes full circle. Ruth was ultimately praised for the faithful love she lived out toward Naomi, and she was remembered for her faithfulness. Naomi returned to Bethlehem empty, but her life became full because of Ruth. Though Ruth could not have known how her actions would inspire future generations, by living out the faithful love of God, Ruth shaped the trajectory of Israel and was remembered in the lineage of Jesus (Matthew 1:5).

Questions for Discussion

1. Famine is a key issue in Ruth that moves this small family from Bethlehem to Moab and then back again. Famine appears in various places in the story of Israel (e.g., Gen 12:10–20; 26:1–11). In what ways do you think God provided during these seasons of famine? How has God perhaps met your needs during your own times of scarcity?
2. Does the generosity of Boaz surprise you in Ruth 2? If so, in what ways?
3. Ruth 2 illustrates the faithful love of God being revealed through this small community in Bethlehem. Have you ever experienced the love of God through others in your life and community? Has the love of God ever surprised you in unexpected places and ways? If so, how was this love revealed to you?

Bibliography

Eskenazi, Tamara Cohn and Tikva Frymer-Kensky. *Ruth: The JPS Bible Commentary*. Philadelphia: The Jewish Publication Society, 2011.

Melton, Brittany. *Where Is God in the Megilloth? A Dialogue on the Ambiguity of Divine Presence and Absence*. Leiden, Netherlands: Brill, 2018.

Queen-Sutherland, Kandy. *Ruth and Esther. Smyth and Helwys Bible Commentary*. Macon, GA: Smyth and Helwys, 2016.

Tolkien, J. R. R. *The Hobbit, or There and Back Again*. New York: Random House, 1982.

6. GOD'S STEADFAST LOVE TOWARD DAVID

2 SAMUEL 7:12–16

KEVIN MELLISH

The Davidic Covenant in Context

The pericope of 2 Samuel 7:12–16 is embedded within the larger narrative pertaining to the establishment of God's covenant with David and his offspring (vv. 1–17). Although the term "covenant" (*berit*) never appears in this context, the basic elements of a promissory agreement are evident, particularly in verses 8–16: God identified benevolent actions performed on behalf of David and the people of Israel (vv. 8–9a); God promised to provide a place/land for God's people so they could safely dwell in it (vv. 9–11); and God vowed to raise up offspring to succeed David and to establish the throne of David's family forever (vv. 11–16). Closer inspection of these verses additionally reveals the unconditional nature of this covenant since the obligation fell primarily on God, and not David or his descendants, to fulfill the stipulated guarantees. As such, the Davidic covenant differed markedly from the Mosaic (Sinai) covenant in that the latter was framed as a conditional obligation on the part of the Israelites, with specific forms of punishment outlined for a breach of the terms (Deuteronomy 28:15–46)—even up to and including the loss of land (i.e., captivity). The Davidic covenant, conversely, pledged God's ongoing support for Davidic kingship because God refused to withdraw God's steadfast love for David's household even when a member of David's family committed iniquity.

The specific terms of God's eternal promise to David and his family were set within verses 12–16. In order to comprehend the nature of this agreement more fully, it is first necessary to examine the preceding material in verses 1–11. Verses 1–3 set the initial stage for the covenant with the notice that David desired to build God a house, or temple (*bayit*). In the ancient Near East, it was customary for a king to build a temple in honor of the god/s who provided military and political success. David was no different in that he wanted to construct a temple for God in which the "ark of God" could be placed (v. 2, NRSV). Since the ark of the covenant represented the presence of God, depositing the sacred object in the temple would transform the structure into

God's abode—or, the place where God dwelled on earth.[1] Moreover, the temple would be situated next to the king's palace, thereby illustrating the close and unique relationship between God and king. The proximity between temple and palace conveyed the theological notion that the presence of God resided with and guided the king as he ruled over the people as God's special envoy.

By all accounts, David's intentions appear honorable and, one would think, pleasing to God. David even received approval from the prophet Nathan, who instructed David: "Go, do all that you have in mind; for the LORD is with you" (v. 3, NRSV). Ironically, and somewhat shockingly, God immediately struck down David's idea of building God a house; verses 4–7 provide a stern rebuttal. In an interesting turn of events, God not only put the kibosh on David's building program, but the abrupt response also spoke against God's desire for a temple altogether (vv. 6–7). God reminded David of two important facts that provided justification for the negative reply: 1) God dwelled in a tent/tabernacle as the people of God moved from Egypt to Canaan (v. 6), and 2) God never instructed Israel's leaders to construct a temple (v. 7). In sum, God did not want, need, or ask for a temple to be built. God's rejection of David's proposal, however, set the stage for the plans God had in mind for David and his family.

In recounting God's intentions for David in verses 8–11, the text draws attention to three important elements that served as the foundation of God's covenant with David. God would first make David's name great, "like the name of the great ones of the earth" (v. 9, NRSV). This language suggests David's name and reputation would become well known and well regarded through the success God granted him. The fact that this would be God's doing contrasted with the people of Babel, for example, who attempted to make their name great through their own hubris and striving (see Genesis 11:1–

1. God's presence symbolically rested on the outstretched arms of the cherubim above the mercy seat.

9). Secondly, God ensured that God's people would have a place/land where they could dwell safely as a result of God giving David rest from his enemies (2 Samuel 7:10–11). As David experienced military victory over the surrounding nations and expanded the boundaries of his kingdom, the people would enjoy God's blessing as they lived securely in the land God promised Israel's ancestors. Finally, God declared that David would produce offspring (v. 11) who would come after him to ensure that David's family line and kingdom would continue into perpetuity.

It is important to point out here that the promise to acquire a great name, gain possession of land, and procure offspring in verses 8–11 mirrors the very elements of God's promissory covenant with Abraham. In the ancestral complex, Abram/Abraham migrated to an unknown land with the promise that God would make his name great (Genesis 12:2); he traversed the land of Canaan, which God promised to bequeath to him and his family (Genesis 12:6–7; 13:14–15; 15:18–21; 17:8); and he was guaranteed numerous progeny as his altered name, Abraham (which means "father of a noisy multitude"), implied (Genesis 17:5). As such, the similarities between the two covenantal texts are not coincidental. Both are intended to be read in relationship to one another as David fulfilled, through his accomplishments, the promises made to Israel's ancestors.[2] Such a reading points to and underscores the greatness of the Davidic monarchy as the Israelites realized their long-awaited hopes and dreams during his reign.

Regarding the promise of descendants in 2 Samuel 7:11, God's designs were wrapped up in a carefully crafted pun on the word "house" (*bayit*). God reversed David's plan to construct God a house and in turn directed it toward David and his family with the promise that God would build David a house (*bayit*). The reference did not

2. The land promised to Abram's descendants in Genesis 15:18–21, for example, corresponds to the boundaries of the kingdom of David and Solomon as a result of David's conquests (see 2 Samuel 8:1–14).

imply God would construct David a *physical* structure, such as a palace (we know from verse 2 he already lived in one); instead, it spoke of God establishing a ruling dynasty that would endure throughout the course of time. In the ancient world, royal/dynastic families were customarily referred to as "a house"—a designation that would typify David's family as well.

This promise is not only spelled out in the text under investigation, but it has also been confirmed in extrabiblical sources. Archaeologists have recovered the Tel Dan inscription, which dates to the ninth century BCE, about a century after the time of David. The inscription contains the words of Hazael, the ruler of Syria (842–800 BCE), in celebration of his victory over the territories of Israel and Judah. The relevant portion of the inscription reads as follows: "I put [Jehoram], son of [Ahab] and ruler of Israel, and [Ahaz]iahu, son of [Jehoram] and ruler of *the house of David*, to death."[3] The words of Hazael thus attest to the historical reality of a family line descending from David that ruled in the region of Syrio-Palestine—a tangible confirmation of God's promise to make David a house in verse 11.

The parameters of God's promise to build a house for David are set out in more detail in verses 12–16. Verse 12 brings the issue of a house into greater focus because it anticipates the end of David's life: "when your days are fulfilled and you lie down with your ancestors" (v. 12, NRSV). Although this notice speaks of David's death, it does not signal the end of David's line; the promise of descendants is stated in the second half of the verse: "I will raise up your offspring (*zera*) after you, who shall come forth from your body" (NRSV). This statement appears to refer to David's family and his ensuing dynasty. The Hebrew word for offspring (*zera*) in verse 12 is a singular noun that has a collective meaning. It is usually translated as "seed" because it can refer to the type of seed one plants in the ground, or it

3. Victor H. Matthews and Don C. Benjamin, *Old Testament Parallels: Laws and Stories from the Ancient Near East*, rev. and exp. ed. (New York: Paulist Press, 1997), 161.

connotes the reproductive seed of men that is transferred during sexual intercourse. By extension, the term has a collective meaning and is often rendered as "offspring," as is the case here. As a collective noun, though, the plural aspect is still inherent within it; thus, it can also be translated as "descendants."

However, the collective/plural understanding of the term stands in contrast with the last clause of verse 12, which speaks of an individual person: "and I will establish *his* kingdom" (NRSV, emphasis added)—the masculine singular pronoun modifies the word "kingdom." Moreover, verses 13–15 continue to speak of an individual (Solomon, specifically, since the building of the temple he would build is mentioned in verse 13, although he is never mentioned by name).

To be sure, the Old Testament does contain instances when the term *zera* can refer to an individual child. For example, after Eve gave birth to Seth she announced: "God has appointed for me another child (*zera*) instead of Abel" (Genesis 4:25, NRSV). Hannah prayed that God would give her a child (*zera*), and in return she promised to "give *him* to the LORD for all the days of *his* life" (1 Samuel 1:11, NIV, emphasis added). In Genesis, Abram remonstrated that he did not have a child (*zera*) and that his servant, Eliezer, would inherit his household (Genesis 15:3, 5). Based on this analysis of *zera*, the collective and singular sense of the term are in play in 2 Samuel 7:12 as the perspective shifts between the descendants of David on the one hand and his immediate heir on the other. The future and the present are both in view.

The promise of offspring is fortified by the notice of God's unending love and support for David's family (vv. 14–16). The special relationship God developed with David would be continued through his progeny. God would relate to the child as a father relates to a son: "I will be a father to him, and he shall be a son to me" (v. 14, NRSV). The father-son imagery is not intended to be taken literally, as though God begat the son, but it functioned as an analogy that spoke to the intimate relationship between God and his anointed. In ancient times, kings were often referred to as the deity's son because they were viewed as empowered to rule on behalf of the god. A similar concept can be found in the Old Testament, especially in Psalm 2. Psalm 2 is a prayer/song in support of God's anointed (i.e., the king), and it tells of God's close relationship to him: "I have set my king on Zion, my holy hill . . . [The LORD] said to me, 'You are my son; today I have begotten you'" (vv. 6, 7, NRSV). This excerpt bears witness to the unique bond God formed with the king who enjoyed divine sponsorship and could expect God's succor in times of trouble (vv. 2–5, 8–9).

The parameters of God's devotion to the Davidic king are spelled out more fully in 2 Samuel 7:14–16. These verses speak of the *radical* nature of God's ongoing, unconditional love for David's house. This idea is evident in the fact that God's *hesed* (see below) is not contingent on the faithfulness of the Davidic king since it is assured unconditionally. To be clear, God would mete out judgment in the case of disobedience: "When he commits iniquity, I will punish him with a rod such as mortals use" (v. 14, NRSV). The threat of divine judgment is mitigated, however, by the pledge to remain true to God's covenantal promise: "*But* I will not take my steadfast love [*hesed*] from him, as I took it from Saul" (v. 15, NRSV, emphasis added). The implication of this statement is that David could always expect God to honor the terms of the covenant because God's love for David would not be withdrawn under any circumstance.

The idea of covenant faithfulness is tied to the Hebrew word *hesed* in verse 15. This word is pregnant with meaning and can be translated in many different ways. In a general sense, the term connotes the idea of goodness or kindness. When used in the realm of human relationships it can refer to the kind actions one displays toward another, such as doing favors or extending benefits (see 1 Samuel 20:15; 2 Samuel 16:17). Inherent within the term is the idea of extending goodness toward the lowly and needy (see Proverbs 11:17), which conveys the notion of mercy (see Proverbs 20:28; Job 6:14). In terms of one's relationship to God, it can refer to fidelity and thus be understood as one's love for God, or piety (Jeremiah 2:2; Hosea 6:4).

The term also testifies to God's good and gracious actions on behalf of creation and the people of Israel. Instances of God's *hesed* include redemption from enemies or distress (Genesis 19:19; Exodus 15:13); rescuing one from death (Psalms 6:4; 86:13; Job 10:12); redemption of sin (Psalms 25:7; 51:1); or the kindness and mercy God extends to humans (Genesis 24:27; Psalms 25:10; 40:11–12). As such, it is often translated as "goodness," "loving-kindness," or "mercy." The term becomes especially meaningful when it occurs in the context of covenant relationships, however. As an element of covenant obligation, it connotes the idea of fidelity or faithfulness, "a mode of behavior that arises from a relationship defined by rights and obligations. . . . When *hesed* is attributed to God, it concerns the realization of the promises inherent in the covenant."[4] From this perspective, *hesed* speaks of God's dependable, trustworthy character by which God faithfully adheres to the terms and responsibilities set forth in the covenant relationship.

God's unconditional support for David and his house is further encapsulated in the language of 2 Samuel 7:16. As the capstone of this smaller unit (vv. 12–16), the text emphasizes the *permanent* nature of this contract. In verse 16 God declared that David's "house and your kingdom shall be made sure forever [*olam*] before me" (NRSV). The Davidic covenant thus represented an eternal pledge between God and David's family. The permanent nature of this agreement was reminiscent of God's covenant with Noah and all creation, when God promised never to destroy to earth again so that nature and humanity could survive (Genesis 9:9–17). The second part of verse 16 reemphasized this aspect of the covenant by stating that David's "throne shall be established forever [*olam*]" (NRSV). In examining the terms of the

---

4. H. J. Stoebe, "Hesed," *Theological Lexicon of the Old Testament*, vol. 2, ed. Ernst Jenni and Claus Westermann, trans. Mark E. Biddle (Peabody, MA: Hendrickson, 1997), 449–64.

Davidic covenant, therefore, God assured David that his house and monarchy would never end. David would never fail to have one of his descendants sit on the throne to govern his eternal kingdom.

The Davidic Covenant at Work in the Old Testament

The history of the people of Israel and Judah, as recorded in the books of Kings, is where the fundamental elements of this covenant agreement played out in real time. To be sure, the promise to David was put to the test by his descendants at various stages of Israel's story. A cursory overview of the historical books demonstrates that God lived up to the terms set forth in the covenant arrangement, even when the Davidic king did not remain faithful to God. The unconditional nature of the relationship is specifically alluded to in the reigns of three Davidic kings: Solomon, Abijam, and Jehoram. A brief examination of their reigns provides a better understanding of how God's covenant with David operated in history.

Solomon's story contains a mixture of both good and bad elements. On the one hand, God blessed Solomon with astounding wisdom (1 Kings 3:3–15), and the narratives in 1 Kings 3–10 detail how Solomon's wisdom brought honor, glory, and wealth to the king and the nation. The high point of Solomon's reign was found in the construction and dedication of the Jerusalem temple (1 Kings 5–8), not in his ability to judge difficult cases (3:16–28), nor his engagement in maritime and overland trading ventures (9:26–28; 10:11–12, 26–29). Canonically speaking, chapters 5–8, which center on the resourcing, building, and dedication of the temple, occur in the heart of Solomon's story. By structuring the narratives about Solomon in this fashion, the writers and editors indicate that the temple was Solomon's greatest achievement since it served as the religious epicenter of Judah for the next four hundred years. The completion of the temple also stressed the fulfillment of God's Word to David in 2 Samuel 7:13, which indicated that David's son would build God a house (*bayit*). Solomon, in his dedicatory address, acknowledged as much when he said, "The LORD said to my father David . . . 'Your son who shall be born to you shall build the house for my name.' Now the LORD has upheld the promise that he made" (1 Kings 8:18a, 19b–20a, NRSV).

Solomon's story also contains a tragic ending. First Kings 11:1–8 reminds the reader that Solomon took many foreign wives, and as a result his heart turned after the gods of the nations. Solomon's apostasy engendered God's anger, and God punished the house of David for his disobedience. As promised in the terms of the covenant, though, God may punish David's family, but God would not remove his steadfast love (*hesed*) for David. Faithfulness to the covenant was found in God's word to Solomon after his disobedience: "I will surely tear the kingdom from you and give it to your servant. Yet for the *sake of your father David* I will not do it in your lifetime" (vv. 11b–12a, NRSV, emphasis added). Although judgment would come on David's house in the form of a divided nation, God spared Solomon from witnessing this event because of God's obligation to David.

Solomon, however, did encounter various adversaries as a result of his sin. Not only did God raise up Hadad the Edomite (vv. 14–22) and Rezon of Aram (vv. 23–25) to torment Solomon, but strife also rose up within Solomon's administration. Jeroboam, one of Solomon's officials, rebelled against the king (v. 26). The prophet Ahijah later informed Jeroboam that Solomon's kingdom would be divided and that he would become the leader of the ten tribes of Israel. Ahijah, however, declared on behalf of the LORD that the tribe of Judah would remain with the house of David "*for the sake of my servant David* and for the sake of Jerusalem. . . . Yet to his son I will give one tribe, so that my servant David may always have a lamp [*nir*] before me in Jerusalem" (vv. 32, 36, NRSV, emphasis added). The ten northern tribes eventually seceded from Davidic rule and established the kingdom of Israel in the days of Rehoboam, just as the LORD proclaimed through Ahijah (12:12–19). Because of God's faithfulness to the covenant, however, David's family retained control of Judah despite the rebellion of the northern tribes.

God's promise to David is also attested in the reign of Abijam, a king noted for doing evil in the eyes of God (15:1–8). Abijam continued the evil ways of his father, Rehoboam. The text notes that he "committed all the sins that his father did before him; his heart was not true to the LORD his God, like the heart of his father David" (v. 3, NRSV). A review of the religious revival that took place during the reign of his son Asa indicates that Canaanite worship had taken hold in the kingdom and flourished during the reigns of Rehoboam and Abijam (vv. 9–15). Although Abijam's actions displeased God and he received a negative evaluation in the text, God's faithfulness to David's family remained firm. The text asserts, "Nevertheless *for David's sake* the LORD his God gave him a lamp [*nir*] in Jerusalem, setting up his son after him" (v. 4, NRSV, emphasis added). The imagery of a lamp (as in 11:36) indicated that there would be a representative of David on the throne and that an heir would follow in his place. Like a lamp that continues to burn, Davidic rule would not be extinguished, even though David's descendants sinned against God.

Direct reference to the Davidic covenant showed up again in the reign of King Jehoram, roughly seventy years after King Abijam (2 Kings 8:16–24). Jehoram likewise did evil in the sight of the LORD and, the text claims, "walked in the way of the kings of Israel, as the house of Ahab had done" (v. 18, NRSV). The reference to walking in the way of Israelite kings and the house of Ahab is unique—it occurs only in reference to Jehoram.[5] This is not by accident, however, since his father, Jehoshaphat, sealed an alliance with the household of King Ahab through the arranged marriage of Jehoram and Athaliah, the daughter of Ahab and Jezebel (see 1 Kings 22:2; 2 Kings 8:18, 26). As such, this evaluation accentuates the evil he committed,

---

5. The evaluations of King Ahaz (2 Kings 16:3) and King Manasseh (2 Kings 21:3) come close to this language, but they are not identical to the statement made about Jehoram.

as though his actions resembled the bad behavior associated with Ahab's family.

To review, Ahab and Jezebel were known devotees of the Canaanite god Baal, and they gave state sanction to the worship of this deity by constructing a temple to Baal in Samaria, the capital of the northern kingdom (1 Kings 18:31–32). In addition, Jezebel persecuted the prophets of God as she actively sought to destroy them (1 Kings 18:3–4; 19:1–3). Thus, for Jehoram to be compared to the legacy of his mother- and father-in-law is quite the moral statement—and no other Judean king is afforded this distinction! Nonetheless, despite this dour evaluation, the text proclaimed, "*Yet* the LORD would not destroy Judah, *for the sake of his servant David*, since he promised to give a lamp [*nir*] to him and to his descendants forever" (2 Kings 8:19, NRSV, emphasis added). Even with the great evil Jehoram committed, God preserved David's line and did not remove the kingdom of Judah from Davidic rule. Ironically, the house of David was threatened by Athaliah, the wife of Jehoram, who sought to wipe out the royal family. Her attempts were thwarted, however, when Jehoash, a scion from the line of David, was rescued through the heroic actions of his sister, Jehosheba, and the bold efforts of the priest, Jehoiada, to preserve the life of the child-king (2 Kings 11:1–8). Athaliah eventually met her demise, and with her destruction, the threat to David's family died as well (vv. 13–16).

The Davidic covenant remained intact and operational throughout the four-hundred-year history of the kingdom of Judah. To be clear, the house of David had its share of evil kings who committed all manner of religious and social atrocities. Through it all, a Davidic king remained on the throne, and the house of David retained control of the territory of Judah, just as God promised to David through the prophet Nathan. History would bear out, though, that the kingdom of David would not survive in perpetuity, thus raising important theological questions about the God who established this eternal covenant and how it was to be understood in the wake of the collapse of the house of David.

Reimagining the Davidic Covenant after the Collapse of the House of David

The house of David faced various internal and external threats during its existence yet continued to survive. As a result, the people of Judah came to falsely believe that God would always protect the Davidic king and Jerusalem, God's holy city. They even witnessed how God delivered the king and city in the days of Ahaz (2 Kings 16:5–9; Isaiah 7:14–16) and Hezekiah (2 Kings 18:13–37; 19:32–33; Isaiah 37:33–35) when they faced perilous threats. The people would eventually learn the painful lesson, however, that God would not always intervene to rescue the Davidic ruler, as the end of 2 Kings attested.

Second Kings 25:1–21 recounted the tragic events that brought an end to the Davidic dynasty. Despite the pious actions of King Josiah and the great religious revival he enacted throughout the land, the kingdom of Judah fell shortly after Josiah's death (23:1–25). Even a righteous king like Josiah could not stave off the destruction of Jerusalem—the text pointed out that the sins of Manasseh proved to be too overwhelming in the long run. The text ultimately blamed Manasseh for the destruction of Jerusalem, the temple, and the deportation of the Davidic king in 586 BCE (21:10–15; 23:26–27; 24:3–4). Not only did the Babylonians take Jehoiachin into captivity earlier (597 BCE), but his appointed successor, Zedekiah, was taken prisoner by Babylonian officials, forced to watch as they killed his sons, and later died in captivity (25:1–7). With the Babylonian exile, the line of Davidic kings came to an end and, with it, the seeming annulment of the Davidic covenant. Such harsh realities caused bewilderment among the community and prompted serious theological questions in the face of this existential crisis.

The shock of the collapse of the Davidic dynasty was captured poignantly in the latter part of Psalm 89, a psalm that celebrated the establishment of God's covenant with David (vv. 19–26) and reiterated the enduring nature of the promise (vv. 28–37) but also lamented God's rejection of the Davidic king (vv. 38–51). The psalm ended on a bitter note, with the writer recounting this painful and shocking reality in verses 38–45 and 49–51 (NRSV):

> But now you have spurned and rejected him;
> you are full of wrath against your anointed.
> You have renounced the covenant with your servant;
> you have defiled his crown in the dust.
> You have broken through all his walls;
> you have laid his strongholds in ruins.
> All who pass by plunder him;
> he has become the scorn of his neighbors.
> You have exalted the right hand of his foes;
> you have made all his enemies rejoice.
> Moreover, you have turned back the edge of his sword,
> and you have not supported him in battle.
> You have removed the scepter from his hand,
> and hurled his throne to the ground.
> You have cut short the days of his youth;
> you have covered him with shame.
>
> Lord, where is your steadfast love of old,
> which by your faithfulness you swore to David?
> Remember, O Lord, how your servant is taunted;
> how I bear in my bosom the insults of the peoples,
> with which your enemies taunt, O LORD,
> with which they taunted the footsteps of your anointed.

The writer of this psalm claims God rejected the anointed one (i.e., messiah) and renounced the covenant with David. This psalm is uniquely positioned within the structure of the Psalter because it closes out Book III. Scholars have noted that the Psalter is organized into five major sections, which collectively retell the story of the people of God.[6] The end of Psalm 89 is meant to correspond to the tragic events of 586 BCE, when the Babylonians destroyed Jerusalem and took the Davidic king into captivity. Such actions seemingly spelled the end of David's dynasty, a reality that subsequent history proved true. This catastrophic experience caused the community to grapple seriously with the meaning of these events and wrestle with the dissonance between God's eternal promise to David and the realities of a future with no Davidic ruler. How were the people to understand this covenant now that the Davidic king was taken into exile and the dynasty had come to an end? How could God possibly deliver on the promises made to David and his family when the people found themselves in exile and under the thumb of a foreign government? How could they envision the covenant when Davidic kingship failed to materialize in the post-exilic period?

Even though the king and people suffered the destruction of Jerusalem and were led into Babylonian captivity, a flicker of hope remained for David and his family. The book of 2 Kings ended on a positive note that implied the possibility of a future for David's family. Second Kings 25:27–30 in particular includes the account of the release from prison of King Jehoiachin, whom the Babylonian king subsequently allowed to dine at his personal table.[7] Although Jehoiachin was never mentioned after the account in 2 Kings, the text underscored the fact that a remnant from David's family survived into exile. That the editors of 2 Kings included this information to close out the book provides evidence that they considered a future with a restored Davidic monarchy to be plausible.

---

6. V. Steven Parrish, *A Story of the Psalms: Conversation, Canon, and Congregation* (Collegeville, MN: Liturgical Press, 2003).

7. Administrative documents of Nebuchadnezzar II mention Jehoiachin, along with other men from Judah, receiving their allotment of oil in Babylonia. See James B. Pritchard, ed., *The Ancient Near East: An Anthology of Texts and Pictures*, vol. 1 (Princeton, NJ: Princeton University Press, 1973), 205.

Events at the end of the exilic period also intimated a future with a Davidic leader. At the beginning of Ezra, the text recounted that Cyrus, the Persian king, declared the people of Judah could return home to rebuild their lives and their temple (1:2–4). Listed among the group of early returners to Judah was Sheshbazzar, who was called the "prince of Judah" (v. 8, NRSV). The reference to Sheshbazzar as the prince of Judah indicated that he descended from the line of David and potentially from Jehoiachin directly (see 1 Chronicles 3:18). Although Sheshbazzar represented the possibility of the restoration of Davidic leadership among the community, he quickly disappeared from the text after Ezra 1, with no explanation given for his absence.

Although this disappearance may seem to have spelled the doom of David's family once again, the text then introduced Zerubbabel, another descendant of David, at the beginning of the very next chapter! Not only did the appearance of Zerubbabel among a second list of returners indicate the preservation and continuation of David's line, but his presence in Judea also injected new hope among the people that Davidic leadership had been restored (2:1–2). Zerubbabel even appeared to have fulfilled an important political role among the people because he was instrumental in leading the people in rebuilding the altar and reestablishing the foundation for the second temple. Moreover, the prophet Haggai referred to Zerubbabel as God's "signet ring," a traditional symbol of royal authority (Haggai 2:23). Just like others who wore the king's signet ring in ancient times (Genesis 41:42; Esther 3:10), Haggai envisioned Zerubbabel as one who would govern with the authority of a monarch. With Zerubbabel, therefore, the Davidic covenant appeared to have survived with God preserving a remnant from David's family in the aftermath of the exile. This hope was short-lived, however, and any prospects for a restored Davidic kingdom were quickly dashed. Zerubbabel, like Sheshbazzar, disappeared suddenly from the text and from history, and God's promise to David appears to have vanished as well.

In the wake of these changing fortunes, the community had to wrestle with the question of how to understand the Davidic covenant since Davidic kingship never rematerialized from the exilic period onward. As the people thought over this difficult reality carefully, they formulated different responses to address the theological conundrum it presented. In order to make sense of the Davidic covenant under these circumstances the biblical writers and editors were, first of all, forced to rethink the unconditional nature of the promise. Considering what had happened to David's family in history, maybe the eternal nature of the Davidic covenant really did depend on the faithfulness of David's heirs. This sentiment is evident in 1 Kings 2:2–4, where the writers and/or editors responsible for the story of David and Solomon revised the unconditional element of the covenant as they recounted the events surrounding the transition from David to Solomon. This text, scholars believe, derived from a period after the exile occurred, and the fall of the Davidic dynasty is presupposed. Consider David's words to Solomon in vv. 2–4 (NRSV):

> I am about to go the way of all the earth. Be strong, be courageous, and keep the charge of the LORD your God, walking in his ways and keeping his statutes, his commandments, his ordinances, and his testimonies, as it is written in the law of Moses, so that you may prosper in all that you do and wherever you turn. Then the LORD will establish his word that he spoke concerning me: 'If your heirs take heed to their way, to walk before me in faithfulness with all their heart and with all their soul, [then] there shall not fail you a successor on the throne of Israel."

In this text, David provided instruction to Solomon as Solomon prepared to take the throne. Note that the speech by David stressed careful *obedience* to God's instruction, taking a form that mirrored God's speech to Joshua as he readied to lead the people after Moses (Joshua 1:7–9). It is particularly noteworthy, however, that the Davidic promise was recast with a conditional "if," so that the permanence of the Davidic kingdom is *dependent* on careful adherence to the Torah!

A similar phenomenon occurred in Solomon's dream theophany at Gibeon in 1 Kings 9:2–9. This account represented the second time God appeared to him in a dream at Gibeon (see 3:1–15). In this second vision, God spoke to Solomon after the dedication of the temple was complete, alluding to the promise made to David. Like 1 Kings 2:2–4, the language is noteworthy because it nuances the promise from 2 Samuel 7:12–16: "As for you, if you will walk before me, as David your father walked, with integrity of heart and uprightness, doing according to all that I have commanded you, and keeping my statutes and my ordinances, then I will establish your royal throne over Israel forever, as I promised your father David, saying, 'There shall not fail you a successor on the throne of Israel'" (1 Kings 9:4–5, NRSV).

Once again, the Davidic promise was conditionalized. God would ensure the perpetuation of David's kingdom if, and only if, Solomon (and, by extension, the rest of David's offspring) kept God's statutes and commands. Verses 6–10 further broadened the scope of this injunction to include the effects disobedience would have on Israel and the temple as well. If David's descendants turned from God and did not keep God's ordinances, then the people would be removed from the land (v. 7), and the temple would be turned into a "heap of ruins" (v. 8, NRSV). Failure on the part of David's family would bring judgment on all Israel—the exact bitter reality the king and people had experienced in their recent past (Psalm 132:11-12 also conditionalizes the promise).

Another response is detected in the Chronicler's rendition of God's promise to David. First and Second Chronicles was a post-exilic work, dating roughly to around 400 BCE, a time well after the exile was over and the Judean community had been reestablished. In recounting the promise to David in 2 Samuel 7:12–16, the Chronicler reworked the agreement by excising its unconditional elements, focusing the attention on God's house, rather than David's house: "[One of your own sons] shall build a *house* for me, and I will establish his throne forever. I will be a father to him, and he shall be a son to me. I will not take my steadfast love from him, as I took it from him who was before you, but I will confirm him in my *house* and in my *kingdom* forever, and his throne shall be established forever" (1 Chronicles 17:12–14, NRSV, emphases added).

The scope of the promise in Chronicles was narrowed to Solomon's kingdom specifically since he was the one who built the temple for God and since his reign would be established through the construction and enduring presence of that edifice. Solomon (and David's family) nevertheless took a backseat here as the focus of this text shifted its attention to God's house and God's kingdom, which were central to the concerns of the Chronicler. Since the temple served as the main religious center for the people in post-exilic Judea, it is not surprising that the Davidic covenant was reshaped to highlight this reality.

A third way the biblical writers reconfigured the promise to David involved transferring the language of "messiah" from those rulers descending from the line of David to other, non-Israelite candidates. This is particularly apparent in Isaiah 40–54, where the writer spoke of Cyrus, the king of Persia, as God's anointed, or messiah. The prophetic voice began chapter 45 with the notice: "Thus says the LORD to his anointed, to Cyrus" (v. 1, NRSV). Cyrus—a non-Israelite king who did not even know the LORD (YHWH), the God of Israel (see v. 4)—would liberate the Lord's people from Babylonian captivity as the prophet declared (see vv. 13–14). As the Lord's divinely appointed redeemer, he was described in language usually reserved for Davidic kings.

A similar phenomenon occurred again in Isaiah, only in this case the Davidic covenant was reformulated to have been made directly with the people of God: "Incline your ear, and come to me; listen, so that you may live. I will make with you an everlasting covenant, my steadfast, sure love [*hesed*] for David" (55:3, NRSV). According to the prophet, the unconditional love and support God had shown David and his family would be with the people of God as they looked forward to a future free from captivity. In this invitation to covenant life (see vv. 1–11), the prophet declared that God would turn the former covenant with David into one with the whole nation if the people would respond favorably to the call extended to them.

As the history of the Jewish people progressed through the postbiblical period, the community continued to try to ascertain the meaning of the Davidic covenant and what form a Davidic leader or messiah would take. During the intertestamental era (i.e., the period between the Old and New Testaments), different interpretive options emerged. There were those who had not given up on the idea of a restored Davidic kingdom. They considered the words of the prophets of old, which declared God would raise up a branch among David's family who would set up and rule over a just and righteous society (see Isaiah 11:1–9; Jeremiah 23:5–6; 34:14–16; Ezekiel 34:23–24). As the Jews continued to live under the rule of foreign powers (Babylonian, Persian, Greek, Ptolemaic/Seleucid, and Roman) throughout their history, it became obvious to many that a messianic leader would necessarily overthrow these foreign rulers and establish an independent Judean society. This idea culminated many years later in the Bar Kokhba revolt of 132–135 CE, when Simon ben Kosiba, whom Rabbi Akiva hailed as a messiah, led a failed rebellion against the Romans.[8]

Others looked beyond the political realm, believing the messiah would carry out a religious function. This appears to have been a belief among the members of the Dead Sea Scrolls community at Qumran. In addition to a political messiah, manuscript evidence indicated that messianic duties would be shared with a priestly messiah. In

8. The Maccabees also led a revolt (theirs successful) against the Seleucid ruler Antiochus IV in 164 BCE, and reestablished Judean independence during the successive reigns of the Hasmonean rulers, but the Maccabees did not descend from the line of David.

their religious vision for the future, they understood the political messiah to be subject to the authority of his priestly counterpart. In other writings, they envisioned the messiah in an eschatological sense. Not only would this figure herald the coming of God's eschatological kingdom on earth, but—as one who carried the titles "Son of God" or "Son of the Most High"—he would also be endowed with the authority to reign over this everlasting kingdom. In other Jewish writings dating to the first and second centuries CE, the messiah is said to be a preexistent, heavenly figure who would establish a long-term reign, much like the millennium rule of Christ in the book of Revelation.

It was into this religious mix that Christian writers emerged, among these the author of the Gospel of Matthew. For Matthew, who was writing to Jewish Christians, portraying Jesus as the long-awaited messiah was paramount for the purpose of his Gospel. It was not by accident that Matthew began the story of Jesus by including his genealogy—something his audience would have appreciated (1:1–17). In Matthew's genealogical account, Jesus was not only connected to Abraham, the father of the Jewish people, but he was also shown to be a descendant in the line of David. According to his rendition of Jesus's personal history, Matthew showed that it was fourteen generations from David to the Babylonian exile and fourteen generations from the Babylonian exile to Jesus, the Messiah (vv. 16–17). The number fourteen not only had theological significance, since it spoke to Jesus's perfection, but Matthew also used the Babylonian exile to demarcate the time from David to Jesus—the same event that prompted important questions about the future of the Davidic covenant in the first place! By structuring Jesus's personal history in this fashion, Matthew demonstrated that the Israelites no longer lived in religious-spiritual exile and that, more importantly, in Jesus—the son of David and the Messiah—the promises outlined in the Davidic covenant had been fulfilled in a perfect way. Indeed, through Christ, the God of love in the Old Testament made the benefits of the Davidic covenant an eternal reality for all!

Questions for Discussion

1. Has there been a time in your life when you questioned whether God really loved you? What happened to bring you to that point? How did you work through that time?
2. Consider the many centuries through which the people of God waited for the fulfillment of God's promise in the Davidic covenant and wondered what that fulfillment would look like. How do you and your Christian community practice patience as we wait to see how God will fulfill God's promises?
3. Have you experienced times when disappointment and/or confusion over the way things have turned out in your life have caused you to rethink or reevaluate the way God was at work in your situation? How did you gain a new perspective about God and God's purposes for your life after you worked through those experiences?

Bibliography

Matthews, Victor H. and Don C. Benjamin. *Old Testament Parallels: Laws and Stories from the Ancient Near East.* New York: Paulist Press, 1997.

Parrish, V. Steven. *A Story of the Psalms: Conversation, Canon, and Congregation.* Collegeville, MN: Liturgical Press, 2003.

Pritchard, James B., ed. *The Ancient Near East: An Anthology of Texts and Pictures*, vol. 1. Princeton, NJ: Princeton University Press, 1973.

Stoebe, H. J. "Hesed." *Theological Lexicon of the Old Testament*, vol. 2. Edited by Ernst Jenni, with assistance from Claus Westermann. Translated by Mark E. Biddle. Peabody, MA: Hendrickson, 1997.

7. GOD'S EXCLUSIVE LOVE

EZRA 10:10–11

JIM EDLIN

THE BOOKS OF EZRA and Nehemiah pose a special challenge for the discussion of God's love in the Old Testament. If the love of God is characterized as welcoming inclusion that extends open arms to all people everywhere, then the stories in Ezra and Nehemiah do not seem to reflect this trait. Rather, we find an exclusivism that sets up boundaries, pushes people away, and ostracizes them from the community of faith and God. But what if God's love is about more than inclusion? Can God set boundaries and still be loving? Ezra 10:10–11 records the crucial moment when Ezra the scribe commanded the people of God to "separate yourselves from the peoples around you and from your foreign wives" (NIV). Ezra called followers of God to be exclusive, to separate themselves from certain types of people. Apparently not everyone was welcome in the community of faith during Ezra's time. How is this loving? Can this truly reflect the God of Scripture?

Possible Interpretations

The idea of excluding anyone from God's community, as Ezra demanded, feels wrong to many people. It especially offends the sensibilities of modern Western culture, which has taken great pains to promote inclusion at all levels. Everyone must be included. People who set boundaries on communities are viewed as close-minded, old-fashioned, and out of step. In order to deal with the excluding God found in Ezra-Nehemiah, some interpreters might suggest that this feature reflects the Old Testament God of law rather than the New Testament God of grace. They might assume the revelation of two different deities in each testament, or perhaps a change in the character of God. Neither position, of course, is orthodox Christianity, and they run counter to Jesus's own testimony. Jesus said, "Anyone who has seen me has seen the Father" (John 14:9, NIV). The God of the New Testament is in fact the God of the Old Testament revealed in Jesus Christ.

Another approach to dealing with the God of Ezra-Nehemiah is to suggest this depiction reflects tendencies of the God of early Judaism more than the God of Christianity. Throughout the intertestamental period, Judaism showed a marked movement toward distinguishing themselves from surrounding cultures. Groups like the Hasidim, the Essenes, and others pushed Judaism toward isolation from the rest of the world. By New Testament times, Jesus encountered scribes, Pharisees, and priests who seemed very closed off and judgmental of those who were not like them. He clearly did not approve of their perspective (see Matthew 23).[1] So perhaps, these scholars suggest, Ezra-Nehemiah fits within this trajectory of the movement of certain strands of Judaism toward more exclusivistic approaches.

If these interpreters are correct, then we might ask why the books of Ezra and Nehemiah are even in the Christian Bible at all. Do they merely provide interesting history about the Jewish people? Maybe they give us an example of religious fervor gone wrong. Perhaps Ezra and Nehemiah are examples of bad religious leaders who tried to isolate and insulate their people from the surrounding world. Indeed, the voice of God never appears within Ezra-Nehemiah to offer an opinion on their scriptural interpretations. Thus, maybe the community portrayed in Ezra-Nehemiah helps explain why the world so desperately needed Jesus to come and reveal how loving God truly is. Neither of these positions, however, does justice to the canonical unity of Christian Scripture. The Bible quite naturally presents a complex picture of who God is, for God cannot be easily defined. Volumes of theological discussions produced over centuries testify to a God who is knowable yet is not fully known. But noting God's complexity is different from suggesting inconsistency in the godhead

1. In light of the ways that some interpreters have used Jesus's attitude toward the religious leaders of his day to support anti-Jewish attitudes in general, it is important to remember that not every scribe, Pharisee, and priest in Jesus's day was judgmental or the target of Jesus's outrage. This is another reason to reject the second approach sometimes used to deal with the exclusiveness in Ezra-Nehemiah.

or espousing dualism. Therefore, we must seek another path toward understanding Ezra 10:10–11.

Historical Setting

In order to hear this passage well, we need to begin by seeking to understand the historical context from which it speaks. The timeframe for Ezra the person is somewhere in the fourth or fifth centuries BCE. Most scholars feel comfortable placing him in the middle of the fifth century, since the biblical text identifies Ezra as a contemporary of Nehemiah, whose timeframe is clearly indicated in Nehemiah 8:9 and 12:26. Thus, the Persian king Artaxerxes mentioned in Ezra 7 is taken as the first by that name, who reigned from 465–424 BCE. So his seventh year, the year Ezra traveled to Jerusalem and made the demands recorded in our passage, would be about 458 BCE.[2]

Regardless of who ruled Persia during Ezra's time, the more important thing for understanding our passage is the socio-religious context of the Jewish community Ezra confronted. This community was only a few generations removed from the devastating upheaval of the Babylonian exile. The impact of the destruction of Jerusalem, its temple, and kingship in 586 BCE had thoroughly disrupted life for the descendants of Abraham. Thousands of Jews were killed, thousand more became captives in Babylonia, and thousands of others became displaced immigrants in surrounding areas like Egypt.

With the fall of Babylon and the rise of the Persian Empire, Jews began to return to their homeland around 537 BCE. A series of caravans trickled into Jerusalem and adjacent villages over the next several decades, gradually repopulating the region with people of Jewish descent. The first groups undertook the monumental task of

---

2. See Jim Edlin, *Ezra-Nehemiah: A Commentary in the Wesleyan Tradition*, *New Beacon Bible Commentary* (Kansas City, MO: Beacon Hill Press of Kansas City, 2017), 24–25.

rebuilding the temple complex in Jerusalem. Ezra 1–6 describes the struggles and final success of this project. Hostile neighbors as well as limited resources posed significant hurdles. But the burgeoning community in Jerusalem finally celebrated the temple's completion in 515 BCE, a little more than a generation before Ezra arrived in Jerusalem.

According to the book of Esther, another traumatic event for Jews unfolded early in Ezra's lifetime. Though the exact date is hard to pin down, the near annihilation of all Jews recorded in Esther must have taken place during the reign of Xerxes I, who ruled Persia from 486–465 BCE. Total disaster was averted, but the trauma of such an event surely left a profound scar upon Jewish communities throughout the Persian Empire. For some, the attempted genocide proved that appearing too Jewish in a Persian world posed considerable risk. Identification with other cultures in the area seemed prudent, serving as the best protection against being singled out for persecution. Marriage to non-Jews created political and familial bonds that might safeguard one from future attempts at ethnic cleansing.

Ezra went to Jerusalem at the behest of the Persian government not long after the events recorded in Esther. Artaxerxes charged Ezra, as special counsel to the throne concerning Jewish affairs, to go there and instruct people in the laws of their God (Ezra 7:12–26). As strange as this may sound to us today, it was apparently typical Persian policy. We know that first Cambyses, then Darius I, commissioned an Egyptian priest named Udjahorresnet to accomplish a similar mission in his homeland.[3] Contrary to Assyrian and Babylonian policies of previous generations, the Persians empowered subjects within their empire to strengthen local customs, which included religious beliefs. They understood the value of diversity and promoted it throughout their kingdom. Persians undoubtedly recognized the eco-

3. See Joseph Blenkinsopp, "The Mission of Udjahorresnet and Those of Ezra and Nehemiah," *Journal of Biblical Literature* 106 (1987): 409–21.

nomic and political advantages of such a strategy, and their longevity as an empire testifies to its wisdom.

So Ezra found himself among people who were two or three generations removed from the initial days of Jerusalem's recovery and only a few years away from the threat of genocide. The excitement of restoring the Jewish community in Jerusalem had waned while economic and political hardships continually slowed recovery. Much of the fiscal challenge might have come from drought and pest infestation cycles that regularly plagued Israel's agricultural economy. But breakdowns in wider market networks might be associated more with political disenfranchisement from neighboring people. According to Nehemiah 4, Samaritans, Ammonites, Arabs, and others devised numerous plots to undermine advancements in the Jewish community. People like Tobiah the Ammonite and Sanballat the Samaritan likely prospered while Jerusalem's economy remained weak or at least under the control of others. A strong Jewish community apparently threatened their neighbors' positions within the region.

Along with Judah's economic and political struggles, spiritual lethargy had also set in according to the prophet Malachi. His messages, which appear to be contemporary with Ezra and Nehemiah, reveal a Jewish community that was spiritually confused. People were questioning God's interest in the little group in Jerusalem (Malachi 1:2), and whether serving God had any advantages (Malachi 3:14). The grand promises of restoration found in the writings of Isaiah, Jeremiah, and Ezekiel must have seemed illusory. The hope expressed in Jeremiah's vision of "abundant prosperity and peace" in a Jerusalem filled with "the sounds of joy and gladness" apparently seemed like a distant dream (Jeremiah 33:9–11, NIV; see also Isaiah 60:1–22; Ezekiel 36:33–35). Certainly little evidence of its fulfillment could be observed during Ezra's time.

Amidst these realities, compromising beliefs and assimilating to the surrounding culture looked inviting. If a Jewish community were to survive in such an environment, one might assume alternative paths must be taken. Many in the Jewish community in Jerusalem apparently adopted this view. Once Ezra arrived, community leaders told him, "The people of Israel, including the priests and the Levites, have not kept themselves separate from neighboring peoples. . . . They have taken some of their daughters as wives for themselves and their sons, and have mingled the holy race with the peoples around them" (Ezra 9:1a, 2a). The leaders here seem to be extending to their own time older laws such as Deuteronomy 7:1–6, which commanded the Israelites who were entering the promised land of Canaan under Joshua not to intermarry with people outside their community.[4]

These are the circumstances behind Ezra's call to "separate yourselves" in Ezra 10:10–11. If the people of Judah were to realign themselves with the guidelines of Mosaic laws, they must set aside the strategy of survival through assimilation to the surrounding cultures. Instead, they must decide to form a distinctive community of faith that separated itself from the dominant culture. According to Ezra, this formation would entail putting away foreign wives and excluding others from the community of faith.

Grammatical Considerations

In order to clarify further the meaning of Ezra 10:10–11, some analysis of the grammar employed in it and related passages will prove helpful. We need to examine exactly what the community was accused of doing and what Ezra actually said to them. Did he really tell men to divorce their wives just because they were not Jews? That sort of action does not seem to reflect a person who serves a loving God.

4. It is clear from stories elsewhere in the Old Testament that Israelites in other time periods had not applied this older law as strictly as the leaders in Ezra's day were doing (see, for example, Boaz's marriage to Ruth, a Moabite, and the story of the Canaanite woman Rahab in Joshua 2—and note both Ruth's and Rahab's later inclusion in the genealogy of Jesus [Matthew 1:5], which indicates that Rahab also married a descendant of Abraham). See further discussion, especially of Ruth, later in this chapter.

Before looking at Ezra's words, we must return to the accusation made by the Jewish leaders that led to Ezra's radical call for excluding people from the community. The leaders asserted that men "have mingled the holy race with the peoples around them" by marrying foreign women (Ezra 9:2, NIV). The translation "holy race" may be unfortunate here, since it could suggest a racist tendency among the Jewish leaders. Literally, the text reads "the holy seed" (*zera haqodesh*), which actually evokes the language of Israel's covenant with God rather than the language of race. Judah's leaders no doubt had a passage like Leviticus 19:2 in mind, where God called his covenant people to "be holy because I, the Lord your God, am holy" (NIV). This reference to "the holy seed" has to do with the community's covenant relationship to God, not with ethnicity. Their goal was a distinctive community fit for fellowship with a holy God. They were not aiming at a homogeneous racial group.

God warned Israel just before they entered the promised land that "mingling the holy seed with the peoples around them" would be dangerous. It would undermine the spiritual life of the community. Unbelievers would "turn your children away from following me to serve other gods," God told them (Deuteronomy 7:4, NIV; see also Exodus 34:16). Solomon is the prime example of the corrupting effects of such unholy unions (see 1 Kings 11:1–11; Nehemiah 13:26–27). This was what Judah's leaders sought to avoid.

As a result, they labeled these marriages to nonbelievers "detestable practices" (Ezra 9:1, NIV). Later, when Ezra prayed about this issue, he also identified it in the same way (vv. 11, 14). The term translated "detestable practices" (*toevot*) refers to conduct that repulses God. Elsewhere in the Old Testament, the word describes eating unclean food (Deuteronomy 14:3); inappropriate remarriage (Deuteronomy 24:4); ritual prostitution (1 Kings 14:24); idolatry (Isaiah 41:24); child sacrifice (Jeremiah 32:35); and adultery (Ezekiel 22:11), as well as marriage to women who worshiped foreign gods (Malachi 2:11). Ezekiel used the term more than thirty times to describe such things as oppressing the poor, committing adultery, and cheating a person in business (see Ezekiel 18:12). Thus, the problem in Ezra's community was placed in the same category as the kinds of activities that might be most damaging to a social group. Such actions undermined trust and cohesion within the community.

In his prayer of intercession for the Jewish community (9:6–15), Ezra used additional terms to describe marriages to non-Jews. He called them "sins" (*awonot*) and "guilt"-producing (*ashmah*) actions (vv. 6–7, 13, 15). The first term connotes crookedness—that is, bent away from God's design for life. The second describes the status of one who has committed an offense that creates separation between the people and God. According to Ezra, these kinds of actions were the very ones that led Abraham's descendants to lose the land, a seminal sign of Israel's covenant relationship to God (v. 7).

Further, Ezra identified mixed marriages as being "unfaithful" (10:10), a term also used in 9:2, 9:4, and 10:6 to describe these marriages. To be "unfaithful" (*maal*) conveys the idea of deceitful disloyalty toward God, a behind-the-back kind of betrayal of the covenant relationship with God. The term is employed to describe a wife's infidelity toward her husband in Numbers 5:12 and the actions of Achan in Joshua 7:1. Ezekiel also called a righteous person who "turns from their righteousness and commits sin" unfaithful (18:24, NIV).

Instead of acting unfaithfully, Ezra urged his people to do three things: "honor the LORD," "do his will," and "separate yourselves from the peoples around you" (10:11). The call to "honor" God (*tenu todah*) literally translates "give thanks" to the Lord, which suggests confession of sin (see ESV, NASB, NLT). The expression is used regularly throughout the Psalms to invite people to acknowledge God's righteousness and confess their sin in light of it. As we know from the rest of Scripture, confession means more than speaking words. It involves action. In this case, confession entailed doing what God willed and separating from the influence of ungodly wives.

The term "separate" (*badal*) does not necessarily mean divorce, though most commentators assume it does. It primarily means to set something apart from something else. *Badal* is used to talk about distinguishing between such things as the elements of creation (Genesis 1:14), clean and unclean sacrifices (Leviticus 20:25), and Israel and the nations (Leviticus 20–24). It is primarily about making a distinction. As with the term "send away" (*yatza'*), used in Ezra 10:3 and 10:19 to talk about dealing with foreign wives, "separate" could suggest creating different living arrangements rather than enacting legal divorce proceedings. The major issue was separating "from the peoples around" and their ungodly influences. Ezra's primary concern was to preserve a community that remained faithful to God, which would be essential to fostering genuine relationship with God.

This analysis of terms underscores the point that Ezra condemned marriage outside the community of faith in order to maintain a vital covenantal relationship with God inside the community of faith. The issue was not ethnic purity or legalistic observance of law. The problem with these specific marriages was their potential to undermine fellowship with God and fellow believers. Such marriages revealed a spiritual issue in the community. Thus, the call toward exclusivity emerged out of God's loving concern to preserve intimacy with and among God's people. God set boundaries to foster spiritual life.

Immediate Literary Context

The immediate literary context encompasses the four chapters of Ezra 7–10, which relate the story of Ezra's mission to his homeland. The major point of this story is to tell how the restoration of the law of Moses within the community of faith contributed toward the restoration of God's people. As these chapters intend to convey, the law of Moses breathed new life into God's people as they realigned themselves with it and distinguished themselves from surrounding cultures. Thus, the climax of this story comes at the point of our focus passage, Ezra 10:10–11.

Chapter 7 begins the narrative with an introduction to the man Ezra and his commission from the Persian emperor Artaxerxes. The king authorized Ezra to return to Judah and "appoint magistrates and judges to administer justice" according to the laws of Moses (7:25–26, NIV). Once this had been accomplished, the narrator tells us that community leaders reported a violation of the directive regarding relationships with non-Israelites (9:1–2).

The subsequent record of the dramatic reaction of Ezra and the community to this revelation highlights the severity of the violation (9:3–10:9). Marriage to foreign women was no small matter. The narrator details Ezra's anguish as he tore his clothes, pulled his hair, threw himself down, and prayed a passionate prayer of communal confession (9:3–15). In this prayer, Ezra highlighted the specific law violated by alluding to Leviticus 18:25–30 and 20:22–24. He also directly quoted Deuteronomy 7:3, "Do not give your daughters in marriage to their sons or take their daughters for your sons" (Ezra 9:12, NIV), and Deuteronomy 23:6, "Do not seek a treaty of friendship with them at any time" (Ezra 9:12, NIV). The narrator continues to heighten the drama by recording the reaction of community members. They also "wept bitterly" (10:1, NIV), confessed unfaithfulness to God (v. 2), and proposed that they "send away all these women and their children" (v. 3, NIV).

The climactic moment in the story arrives when Ezra announced the remedy for the sin. With the extended community gathered round, Ezra stated the infraction, "You have been unfaithful," and pronounced the verdict, "separate yourselves from the peoples around you and from your foreign wives" (vv. 10, 11). Then the narrator tells us that the assembly agreed with Ezra's judgment and proceeded to execute it. The remainder of the story relates how this took place and even includes a list of violators (vv. 12–44).

The entire narrative of Ezra 7–10 illustrates how a community that restores God's law must distinguish itself from the rest of its world. The Jewish community in Judah may have had other shortcomings with regard to the law of Moses, but this story focuses on the one particular issue of corrupting influence from foreign cultures who worshiped other gods. It underscores the need for God's community to exclude some people in order to be faithful to the LORD and to his laws. Exactly how that exclusion was enacted—what it meant for the women and children involved—is not detailed in Ezra-Nehemiah.

Thus, Ezra 7–10 contributes to the major message in Ezra-Nehemiah about how God graciously renews God's people following the failure of exile. It joins the narratives about restoring the temple (Ezra 1–6), restoring the walls of Jerusalem (Nehemiah 1–6), and restoring covenant commitments (Nehemiah 7–13). These four stories communicate hope for restoration to those whose sin of unfaithfulness to God has elsewhere been identified as causing catastrophic consequences, such as Israel's exile (see 1 Kings 9:6–9; 2 Kings 17:7–20; Jeremiah 16:10–13).

Larger Literary Context

These observations on the literary design of Ezra 7–10 might cause us to wonder if its emphasis on exclusion is a unique element within the overall story of Ezra-Nehemiah. Could Ezra's call for separation be an anomaly within these books? Perhaps the community under restoration became more inclusive on other occasions and the incident in Ezra 7–10 was only a one-time event. A survey through Ezra-Nehemiah, however, reveals this is not the case. The theme of excluding people emerges many more times. In fact, it is a significant element throughout the entire narrative of Israel's restoration after the exile.

The first hint occurs in the early chapters of Ezra when the Jewish community flatly refused the offer from their neighbors of help with rebuilding the temple. The narrator records their unqualified response: "You have no part with us in building a temple to our God" (4:3, NIV). These neighbors—who included Samaritans, Ammonites, and others—seemed to make their offer with good intentions. They said, "We seek your God and have been sacrificing to him since the time of Esarhaddon king of Assyria, who brought us here" (v. 2, NIV). According to accounts in 2 Kings, however, Israel's God was not the only deity they acknowledged. They believed other divine forces must be reckoned with as well, and did not hold that the temple in Jerusalem was the sanctuary of the one and only true God (see 2 Kings 17:24–33).

Once the temple was complete and dedicated, the narrative records a Passover celebration in which non-Israelites joined the exiles. It specifically notes, however, that only those who "separated themselves from the unclean practices of their Gentile neighbors in order to seek the LORD" could participate in this feast (Ezra 6:21). This followed directives given in the laws of Moses about non-Israelite participation in this festival (see Exodus 12:48–49 and Numbers 9:14).

The theme of separation from surrounding cultures continued in the book of Nehemiah. Like Ezra, Nehemiah told those who offered to help the Jews rebuild Jerusalem's walls, "You have no share in Jerusalem or any claim or historic right to it" (2:20, NIV). For several chapters Nehemiah recalled the hostility between the Jews and their neighbors during the wall-building project (see Nehemiah 4–6). He refused to meet with Samaritan, Arab, and Ammonite leaders (6:1) and even recorded his prayer for them, which requested that God "turn their insults back on their own heads" and "give them over as plunder" (4:4, NIV).

Once they finished building the wall, the Jews gathered to hear the law read and then to fast and pray (Nehemiah 8–9). As they met to confess their sins, the narrative notes that "those of Israelite descent had separated themselves from all foreigners" (9:2, NIV). At the conclusion of their prayer, many recommitted themselves to covenant with God. This included "all who separated themselves from the neighboring peoples for the sake of the Law of God" (10:28, NIV). Part of this covenant commitment included the vow to refuse to do business "when the neighboring peoples bring merchandise or grain to sell on the Sabbath . . . or on any holy day" (v. 31, NIV).

As the story of Judah's restoration closes in Nehemiah 13, we find additional incidents of exclusion. The narrative describes the situation about a decade after the community dedicated the rebuilt walls of Jerusalem. When Nehemiah returned to Jerusalem for a second term as governor of Judah, he found that non-Israelites had once again joined the community of faith. He discovered that Tobiah, the leader of a powerful family from Ammon, occupied one of the rooms in the temple complex. Undoubtedly, he made significant contributions to the temple and sought to ingratiate himself to the Jews for political and economic reasons. But Nehemiah said, "I was greatly displeased and threw all Tobiah's household goods out of the room" (13:8, NIV).

The narrative records two other incidents of Nehemiah excluding people at this time. Many details are left out of the book, and it is not clear how much Nehemiah's perspectives represented those of the community as a whole (see 13:5)—but, for example, when he discovered some merchants from Tyre had been coming to Jerusalem and selling merchandise on the Sabbath, Nehemiah shut down their operation. He bluntly told them, "If you do this again, I will arrest you" (v. 21, NIV). In response, the narrator records that they no longer came around on the Sabbath. Nehemiah also found that once again some Jewish men had married women from the surrounding cultures. He publicly disgraced these men and expelled them from the Jewish community (vv. 23–27). Even the grandson of the high priest was reprimanded, and Nehemiah boasted, "I drove him away from me" (v. 28, NIV).

Also in the final chapter of Nehemiah we notice how people in Jerusalem read a portion of the law of Moses that declared, "No Ammonite or Moabite or any of their descendants may enter the assembly of the LORD" (Deuteronomy 23:3, NIV). In response, Nehemiah records that they then "excluded from Israel all who were of foreign descent" from worshiping in the temple (13:3). As in the case of marriages to foreign women, the term "foreign descent" must be taken in a religious rather than biological sense. Otherwise the entire line of David would be excluded because of his Moabite great-grandmother, Ruth. The point of excluding "all who were of foreign descent" was to preserve a community that might genuinely worship the Lord. It was not about being racially selective.

So we can see that numerous passages underscore the theme of exclusion in Ezra-Nehemiah. In addition to these individual passages, we might observe that the two main stories about building the temple (Ezra 1–6) and the walls (Nehemiah 1–6) in Jerusalem made a similar point. By its very nature, construction of structures such as these set boundaries that placed people either within or without. In the case of the walls, its stones excluded those who threatened the community from the outside as well as protected those inside its confines. Gatekeepers kept watch on who entered the city, and they closed the gates each night (see Nehemiah 7:1–3 and 13:19–22).

The temple made distinctions between people even more so. From 1 Kings 6–7 and 2 Chronicles 2–4 we learn that the architectural design of the temple gradually excluded more and more people. The closer one came to the holy of holies, where God's presence most fully resided in the ark of the covenant, the fewer people were allowed. Guidelines set forth in Exodus and Leviticus laid out strict standards for those who would serve or even enter the tabernacle (and later the temple) complex (see, for example, Exodus 28 and Leviticus 16). Not everyone was welcome there.[5]

The other two main stories of Ezra-Nehemiah focus on restoring law (Ezra 7–10) and renewing covenant (Nehemiah 7–13). Both affirm that life in the community of faith was not open to everyone. As

5. The provisions for the tabernacle and, later, the temple indicated a belief that, in drawing near to the manifestation of the presence of God, humans risked death. In order to avoid such a fate, priests had to follow the specific provisions laid out by God (see Leviticus 10).

we have noticed, the story of the restoration of law in Judah in Ezra 7–10 led to the dissolution of marriages, which excluded some from family life and their role as spiritual influencers in the family system. Likewise, the renewal of covenant in Nehemiah 7–13 excluded some. The call for covenant required people to make certain commitments to God and the community. Those who did not commit could not fully participate in the corporate worship experience of Judah as outlined in chapter 10. In particular, this included ceasing commercial activity on the Sabbath and providing for the regular operations of the temple (see 10:28–39). Whether the uncommitted could share in other acts of worship at the temple is not clearly delineated in the text. Yet we do notice that Ezra and Nehemiah sought to apply the law of Moses in their context by drawing a circle around the family and the worshiping community. Unfortunately, this application of the law excluded some from full participation in the spiritual life of their community.

Clearly, then, the theme of exclusion stands at the core of Ezra-Nehemiah's message. God's plan to restore the community of faith in Judah included distinguishing them from the rest of their world. Yet alongside this idea we can also notice that the theme of God's all-embracing grace permeates the material as well. In a manner that may seem incongruent to some, God's exclusive demands were set side by side with Ezra and Nehemiah's witness to God's benevolent goodness.

We might first take notice of this theme in a recurring phrase, "the gracious hand of the Lord" (Ezra 7:6, 9, 28; 8:18, 22, 31; Nehemiah 2:8, 18, NIV). Ezra testified that the success of his mission, including safe transport over the treacherous route to Judah, only happened because "the gracious hand of his God was on him" (Ezra 7:9, NIV). Similarly, Nehemiah's task of rebuilding the walls of Jerusalem came about because of God's unmerited favor. Nehemiah confessed that, "because the gracious hand of my God was on me, the king granted my requests" (Nehemiah 2:8, NIV). Then, when the project came to completion, Nehemiah noted that such a monumental task could only be accomplished in such a short time against such enormous opposition "with the help of our God" (Nehemiah 6:16, NIV).

In addition to this key phrase, the narrator of Ezra-Nehemiah regularly reminds readers of divine providence operating behind the scenes of Judah's restoration. In the introduction to this story, we are told that the entire process began because "the LORD moved the heart of Cyrus" to make a decree that favored God's people (Ezra 1:1). The following story of the return of exiles and their rebuilding the temple affirms God's loving, sovereign hand over the entire process. Against all human odds, "they finished building the temple according to the command of the God of Israel and the decrees of Cyrus, Darius and Artaxerxes, kings of Persia" (6:14, NIV). The point of this statement is that God made his people successful by employing the kings of Persia to bless them. This is the purpose of including copies of decrees and letters of these kings within the book (see Ezra 1:2–4; 6:3–12; 7:12–26). They serve as hard evidence of the gracious hand of the Lord.

We can also notice that, even in his prayer of confession in chapter 9, Ezra affirmed the grace of God. As he mourned the sins of his community, Ezra recalled how "the LORD our God has been gracious in leaving us a remnant and giving us a firm place in his sanctuary" (v. 8, NIV). He confessed that "our God has not forsaken us . . . has shown us kindness . . . has granted us new life to rebuild the house of our God and . . . has given us a wall of protection in Judah and Jerusalem" (v. 9, NIV).

The most extended passage highlighting God's gracious character comes in Nehemiah 9. There the community rehearsed their history with God from Abraham to exile. At the core of this confession was an emphasis upon God's "great compassion" toward the people of God throughout their history (Nehemiah 9:19, 27, 31, NIV). In the rebellious wilderness era, in the chaotic settlement period, and in the failure of exile, the people acknowledged that God had not abandoned them. They affirmed the traditional creed that described the Lord as "a forgiving God, gracious and compassionate, slow to anger and abounding in love" (9:17, NIV; see also Exodus 34:7). Though this prayer acknowledged Israel's consistent rebellion and resulting hardships, it concluded by confessing, "You are a gracious and merciful God" (Nehemiah 9:31, NIV).

While the two great themes of grace and exclusion might seem difficult to combine for us today, Ezra and Nehemiah have no problem viewing them together. They present a God whose constant compassion draws people into a community that has boundaries around it. Yet Ezra-Nehemiah stops short of giving us God's response to the specific ways that Ezra and Nehemiah placed boundaries around their community as they sought to interpret the laws of Moses for their own time.

Canonical Reflections

How does the God portrayed in Ezra-Nehemiah correspond to the God found elsewhere in Christian Scripture? Do these books truly tell us about the same God we meet throughout the rest of the Old and New Testament books? One of the most persistent images of God in the Bible is that of one on a mission to save the world, who relentlessly pursues humans for intimate relationship. God's deep desire to bless "all peoples on earth" (Genesis 12:3, NIV) through the descendants of Abraham regularly recurs throughout both the Old and New Testaments. So God constantly invites people, "Return to me, and I will return to you" (Malachi 3:7, NIV), and offers salvation through Jesus Christ to "everyone who believes" (Roman 1:16, NIV).

This welcoming invitation comes with expectations, though. While proclaiming God's mission to the world, the Bible consistently reminds us that God calls people into a relationship that demands a particular kind of lifestyle and character of those who participate. God invites people to be like God, to "be holy . . . as I am holy"

(Leviticus 18:2). Even Jesus—who reached out to prostitutes, tax collectors, and other marginalized people—prayed that his followers would be set apart from their world (see John 17:17). Paul also urged early believers, "Do not be yoked together with unbelievers," and challenged them to "come out from them and be separate" on the basis of Isaiah 52:11 (2 Corinthians 6:14–17). While extending an open invitation to all people, even gentiles, the apostle repeatedly reminded believers that "God did not call us to be impure, but to live a holy life" (1 Thessalonians 4:7, NIV). God expects the redeemed to live differently than the unredeemed.

Thus, the entire canon of Scripture supports the profile of God drawn in Ezra-Nehemiah. The God of great grace also sets boundaries. Though God seeks to include every person, God's vision for communal living will also exclude some. But how do we reconcile a God who is on a mission to save the world with a God who puts up boundaries? Can a God who excludes people from fellowship be called loving? The key to reconciling these seemingly disparate images of God is found in understanding that love is at the heart of all divine action. As John so boldly stated, "God is love. Whoever lives in love lives in God, and God in them" (1 John 4:16, NIV). Divine love drives the essential mission of God to rescue people from the life this world offers and to bring them into a community that can experience the kind of life only God can give. Such a community is different from what people ordinarily know. It distinguishes itself as God's "treasured possession . . . a kingdom of priests and a holy nation" (Exodus 19:5–6, NIV; see also 1 Peter 2:9). That is to say, it becomes a community that uniquely belongs to God so it can function like priests, who help others come before God.

The goal of God's call to be separate from the world is not to fashion a group of well-behaved people. A holy people is essential to God's mission of love for the world, for only holy people have something to offer those who do not know God. They live a redeemed life that operates out of a different set of values, where people endeavor to reflect the love of God and truly care about one another (1 John 4:7–12). Those who seek to live in God's love and thus distinguish themselves from the way humans ordinarily live can truly reach out and draw people into something different than what the world offers.

Therefore, God's love calls people into a distinctive community where the life originally designed for humans at creation can take place. Intimate fellowship with a loving God and other loving humans distinguishes this community, which flourishes in the freedom of forgiveness and grace. This is the kind of community into which God invites all people, but not everyone can enter into it (see Matthew 7:13–14). Only those who willingly separate themselves from the destructive values and lifestyles of this world can fully experience the love of God and his people.

Conclusion

So the call to separation from the world in Ezra-Nehemiah is actually an expression of the love of God. Ezra's demand to put away foreign wives became the community's means toward fulfilling God's loving mission to the world. By separating themselves from those around them, the people of Ezra's time could function as the kind of community into which people could be invited. Life in this community would not be more of the same. It would be a lovingly supportive community ordered by divine law—something radically different from what they might find among their neighbors. Sometimes love requires God to do the difficult thing. According to Ezra and Nehemiah, this was one of those times. The most loving thing God could do was demand the dissolution of unholy unions to preserve the holy character of his people. The future of God's community and, thus, God's mission to the world depended on such a radical corrective measure.

Contemporary readers of these ancient stories must be careful not to read them too literally or apply simplistically the kind of family separation found in this ancient moment to our contexts today. One way contemporary readers can engage these difficult stories from Israel's past is to consider how marriage and unfaithfulness are used as a symbol throughout the Bible. Both by the Old Testament prophets and the New Testament writers, the relationship between humans and God is likened to marriage. The unfaithful are those who worship gods other than the Lord, who seek political alliances in place of trusting in God, or who refuse to uphold the covenant ethic to care for the widow, orphan, immigrant, and the poor in order that they might enrich themselves. The people of God are to separate themselves from (symbolic) marriages to such unholy endeavors, in favor of a marriage to the most holy One who enables us to love one another as God has loved us.

People today often chafe under the call to holiness, to be different, and to adopt a lifestyle that is distinct from the world. We fear that it appears unwelcoming and may exclude some from experiencing God's grace. To be honest, at times overzealous Christians *have* overplayed their hand in this regard, promoting a suffocating legalism. But, in spite of such misguided passion, the essential call of God to be holy remains. A loving God invites people into a distinctive kind of life where divine love draws people into intimate relationships. The Bible unflinchingly and persistently challenges God followers to distinguish themselves from the world. It is the invitation of a passionately loving God who longs to redeem people from the bondage of sin that enslaves them and return them to life in the garden. Out of a great heart of compassion, God invites people to be different in the way they love in the same way that God is different in the way God loves.

Questions for Discussion

1. What circumstances led Jews to marry non-Jews during the time of Ezra?
2. Why did Ezra and the Jewish leaders feel it was so important to dissolve marriages between Jews and non-Jews? How could this action be seen as the demand of a loving God in their context?
3. What type of communal living results from a truly faithful (symbolic) marriage to God in the biblical sense?

Bibliography

Blenkinsopp, Joseph. "The Mission of Udjahorresnet and Those of Ezra and Nehemiah." *Journal of Biblical Literature* #106 (1987).

Edlin, Jim. *Ezra-Nehemiah: A Commentary in the Wesleyan Tradition. New Beacon Bible Commentary*. Kansas City, MO: Beacon Hill Press of Kansas City, 2017.

8. THE LOVE OF GOD IN THE WHIRLWIND

JOB 38–42

STEPHEN RILEY

THE BOOK OF JOB might not seem like an obvious place to look for an example of the love of God in the Old Testament. The concept of God's love does not explicitly occur in the text, and the main thrust of the book is about how a person responds to the reality of suffering. Yet we can find an important understanding of the love of God through reading God's speech in chapters 38–41 and the closing narrative of the book in chapter 42. In order to account for my understanding, I will offer part of my own story that will hopefully give context for how I came to engage the book of Job and see God's love therein. I also want to provide a framework for reading Job in the broader light of Israel's confessions about God throughout Scripture. Finally, I will read the text of Job with an eye toward seeing how it helps us understand God's love.

My Story

Part of the reason I am attuned to the book of Job is that I am forever changed by my dad's death. He died five days after his sixtieth birthday, after a two-year battle with prostate cancer. To say that the event had a significant impact on my life would be a serious understatement. Up to that point, I had lived my thirty years of life in the wonderful shelter of family and church, where all of my experiences taught me to believe God loved and protected the faithful. At the age of fourteen, I committed my life to following God's call to ministry. I attended a Christian university and trained to serve God through the local church. I served the church, I married Sarah, I went to seminary, and our first child was born. However, none of this prepared me for my dad's diagnosis, journey, and eventual death. Following his death, I began to wonder why my father had died so young and whether God had truly loved him. I asked difficult questions that had no easy answers, such as why God had not healed my dad when my mother, who dearly loves God, fasted and prayed for his healing. The deepest of these questions was how God's love could be truly present in the midst of such overwhelming pain.

As I grieved my dad's death, another experience shaped my life profoundly. A dear friend encouraged me to begin counseling. During this season of my life, I began to lament the loss of my dad and recognize the lack of control I had over the situation. Also during this time, I began a graduate class on Israel's wisdom literature. In that class I was given the opportunity to closely read Israel's texts that focused on what it meant to be wise. Israel's wisdom literature is filled with advice, but it is also written with an eye toward helping the reader learn what it means to be fully human and live faithfully before God. One the first Bibles my parents gave me had an inscription in it from my dad from Proverbs 3:5–6: "Trust in the LORD with all your heart, and do not rely on your own insight. In all your ways acknowledge him, and he will make straight your paths" (NRSV). As I engaged in the wisdom texts in that graduate class, I read the book of Job all the way through in a way I had not done before. Since I read with my father's death in my recent past, the nearness of the text exploded into my life.

Israel's Confessions about God

As a professor of the Old Testament, I often am asked questions about the Bible. A couple years ago, I was helping one of my brothers move across town. One of his friends was also helping and, upon discovering my profession, said, "Oh good, now we can talk about some of that good old fire-and-brimstone, wrath-of-God stuff!" By this time in my life, I have received that kind of well-intentioned reaction enough to not make too much of it. However, it was a reminder that, for many, there is an interpretation of the Old Testament that envisions God as angry, vengeful, and behaving poorly toward humanity.

Such visions are often accompanied by a limited reading of the Old Testament that focuses on certain passages (or certain interpretations of those passages). People who ask me these types of questions generally come from contexts where the interpretive framework for the Old Testament goes something like this: *God created the world and humanity as good, but humans really messed things up. God's wrath and vengeance are poured out on Israel when they continue to sin and fail. Ultimately, the only reason Israel's presence is found in our canon is to point to the New Testament, where we can see the love of God present in Jesus Christ.* In some particularly bad forms of such readings, God's wrath and judgment are understood as central to God's character, as if God being wrathful was what Israel always expected of God. In these readings, the New Testament is presented as the preferred alternative to the Old Testament.

I understood where my brother's friend was coming from. I could see how some interpretations of the Old Testament portraying God as angry or vengeful would be easy to accept. What these readings tend to overlook are the ways God's love has always been present within Israel's scriptures. For example, one of the main theological confessions of the Old Testament is that God is "gracious and merciful, slow to anger and abounding in steadfast love." This confession can be found in Exodus 34:6; Numbers 14:18; Psalms 86 and 103; and Joel 2:13—in addition to numerous allusions in other passages. Israel's point in these texts is that God's relationship with them is primarily based on faithfulness, mercy, and covenantal love—not anger and wrath. It is helpful to note that most of these confessions occur within what are known as revelatory texts. These are the texts in which God reveals Godself to humans. For example, in Exodus 34:6, Israel was responding to God's self-revelation that came following the deliverance from Egypt and the giving of Torah on Mount Sinai. Israel interpreted God's deliverance from bondage and giving of instructions for the new community (Torah) as an act of love.

The Hebrew word used in the confession, *hesed*, which is often translated "steadfast love," is a covenantal word. Through it, Israel understood God to be one who would actively relate to them in a way of fulfilling covenant promises. Alongside this, Israel understood God to be one who was merciful and gracious. In terms of their understanding of how they would relate to God, Israel believed

God's character to be one of covenant faithfulness alongside mercy and graciousness toward them. While there certainly are texts of judgment and portrayals of God's anger, these texts must be read in light of the primary confession of what Israel believed about God. As I continued to grow and reflect on my dad's death, one of the things I could not let go of—both because of my upbringing and because of my training—was the firm conviction that God was in a relationship of love with my dad and my family through our entire journey.

Reading God's Love in Israel's Wisdom Literature

Because Israel's confession of God's love is rooted in God's self-revelation, a group of texts that is often overlooked in the conversation about God's love is the wisdom literature. This oversight happens because of a long interpretive history that focuses on God's self-revelation as manifested in particular saving moments of Israel's past. Unfortunately, Israel's wisdom literature does not contain much reference to such moments, nor does it refer often to Israel's primary confession about God. Thus, the wisdom texts of Proverbs, Job, and Ecclesiastes are often relegated to a side conversation about other matters.

The unfortunate side effects of this are twofold. First, we have simply neglected the wisdom texts far too much in our reading of Scripture; second, when we do read them we often are not looking for ways we can better understand our relationship with God within the larger canonical framework of Israel's confession about God's covenantal love for us. For example, when people read Proverbs, they may primarily read the texts as a way to find guidance for how to be wise in certain situations or to find sayings that will give them a positive outlook for daily life. When reading Job, many people believe the text is primarily a theodicy—that is, a text that helps people understand why God allows bad things to happen to good people.

Unfortunately, this presupposition may take away opportunities to understand these texts in other ways that help us in our desire to live faithfully and understand God's relationship to us in all situations. After my dad died, as I continued in counseling and reading the book of Job, I encountered new possibilities for understanding the reality of suffering and finding hope in the midst of grief. I learned to read the book of Job not as a way of explaining why my dad died but as a way of seeing how suffering and God's presence were intertwined.

Reading God's Love in the Book of Job

The action in the book of Job is kicked off by a question. Twice God asked the adversary, "Have you considered my servant Job?" (1:8; 2:3, NRSV). The adversary had, in fact, and went on to ask God to find out if Job would curse God if suffering came his way (1:9–11; 2:4–5). Alongside God's question, Job was presented as blameless, upright, and a God fearer who shunned evil. The implication of this description was that Job had done nothing to deserve the suffering about to be imposed on him. In the first two chapters, everything was taken from Job in quick succession. Despite this, Job did not curse God; he passed the test. At the end of chapter 2, Job was surrounded by three friends—Eliphaz, Bildad, and Zophar—who sat silently with him because he was in great pain.

If the story ended there, we might be left with a tale about perseverance in the face of great suffering and about how we might comfort one another with our silent presence. However, the book proceeds with another thirty-six chapters of poetic dialogue between Job and his friends. These dialogues feature arguments from Job's friends attempting to convince him that he must have done something to incur his suffering. Eliphaz, Bildad, and Zophar all wanted Job to recognize that God was just; therefore, Job must be in the wrong. They interpreted his suffering from a viewpoint that suffering must be a sign of a lack of God's love or an opportunity to learn something from God. Job refuted their arguments and stated that he must see God to find a way forward.

The type of theology the friends espoused is representative of the same type of reading of the Old Testament that my brother's friend shared with me: that God is primarily concerned with judgment and with meting out suffering. However, the book of Job does not let us get away with that type of reading. The primary descriptions of Job are that he was without fault and that he did not curse God. From the outset, we are told that Job was righteous and that his suffering most certainly did not come because he had done something wrong. Thus, for thirty-six chapters, Job and his friends went round and round trying to articulate their points. The dialogues ended at a stalemate with Job's friends frustrated that he would not admit to doing something to offend God and with Job asking to meet God face to face to argue his case.

Reading Job 38–42

When God finally shows up to speak in chapter 38, we the readers have been patiently listening to the lengthy dialogue between the friends and Job about God's justice and Job's suffering. In fact, one of the points of the dialogue section might be to wear us out with the extended nature of the arguments. We, in effect, are weary and ready for something different by the time God comes on the scene.

Job 38:1–3

Chapter 38 begins with God speaking to Job from the whirlwind (NRSV). However, the term that is translated "whirlwind" fails to do justice to the Hebrew, which could be better understood as "tempest" or "storm." It is a rare word. When it does occur, it is often associated with God and extraordinary events or God's power. For example, in 2 Kings 2:11, it is the word used for that which helps carry Elijah away to heaven. In Isaiah 29:6, the Lord of Hosts is said to visit in a tempest and save the city of Ariel from its enemies. Thus, God answered Job from a place associated with power and salvation.

It is also important to acknowledge that God answered Job—despite Job's friends' arguments that he had done something to offend

God. It is no small thing to acknowledge that God is present in this text and speaking with a human. In wisdom texts, as mentioned before, God's self-revelation was often not at the fore. Since God was present to Job, showing up to answer Job's insistence that he was innocent, it is worth reflecting on how that should affect our interpretation of what happens next.

God's next words (Job 38:2–3) are sometimes interpreted as putting Job in his place. The way they are read is "How dare you question me!" However, in light of the larger context of the book of Job and the fact that God praised Job as one of the greatest humans, it might be worth considering where this interpretation of these verses comes from. Is it possible that our reading of these verses is influenced by something like my brother's friend's understanding of God in the Old Testament? As we come to this passage in Job, are we looking for a God of vengeance when the text is ready to present us with something else? Perhaps these words were instead an invitation for Job. Indeed, it may be that God invited authentic conversation from Job instead of the type of theological dialogue Job's friends gave in the previous thirty-six chapters.

Job 38:4–15

Following these introductory remarks, God began to respond to Job by asking a question (v. 4). Then, for much of chapter 38, God continued to ask questions focused on Job's knowledge of creation. These questions stretch the imagination and force us as readers to interpret their intent. For example, God begins in verse 4 with a seemingly simple question: "Where were you when I laid the foundation of the earth? Tell me, if you have understanding" (NRSV). Most of us understand this to be a rhetorical question, emphasizing that God—and not Job—was the one who created the foundations of the earth. While that may be true, more awaits the perceptive reader. For the next seven verses, God pointed out how beautifully organized the beginning of creation was. This presentation of creation was similar to a view of creation that was common in the ancient Near East. Israel understood that God, specifically YHWH, had created the world by establishing earth on top of chaotic waters and bringing about order and well-being.

This view shows up throughout the poetry of the Old Testament, of which Psalm 104 is a good example. In that psalm, God was depicted as one who set the foundations of the world on the waters and established the order of creation so animals and humans could live by God's good hand. Chaos was removed from creation, and even Leviathan—an ancient symbol of destruction and danger—was understood to be under God's good control (v. 26). Thus, as God established creation, humans were able to flourish. God's question to Job might be understood, then, as not only pointing out that Job was not present at creation but also helping Job understand that God ordered creation in a good way. Therefore, the perceptive reader may be reminded that, even though there may be chaos at the moment, God is the one who created the world and established everything in order. Chaos is no match for the God of Israel.

The next section of the meeting between Job and God (vv. 12–15) has God asking Job if he had power over light and darkness, which is able remove the wicked from the earth (v. 13). This image is reminiscent of Psalm 104:35, where the psalmist asked God to remove the wicked from the earth. Though many readers are disturbed by this seemingly out-of-place verse in the psalm, the request was for God to remove any trace of wickedness from the good order of creation. The image was designed to remind the reader that wickedness was not supposed to have a place in the ordered realm of creation. We readers often take this image to a violent end, but could it be that the psalmist was asking God to remove the wickedness from the sinner? Could it be, as one friend reminded me, that God's power is focused on cleansing people of their sin, rather than cleansing them from the world? This reference could also be God's way of recognizing that Job was still present in creation and so not to be seen as one of the wicked that God was "shaking out" of it. God could have been acknowledging that Job was still the righteous one acknowledged in chapters 1 and 2.

Job 38:16–38

Verses 16–38 highlight God's dominion over the cosmic expanse as God took Job on virtual tour of the world. From the deep sea to the gates of death, from expanses of the skies to hidden places for snow, and from the channels of water in the desert to the clods of dirt caused by rain, Job was shown the far reaches of the universe and the local walking paths. Though, like Job, we have been to all these places, we are taken there as readers and reminded that nothing is beyond the scope of God's care and order. In these various locales, we are also reminded that God often creates and cares for the cosmos in ways that do not fit our categories of good. For instance, verses 25–27 read, "Who has cut a channel for the torrents of rain, and a way for the thunderbolt, to bring rain on a land where no one lives, on the desert, which is empty of human life, to satisfy the waste and desolate land, and to make the ground put forth grass?" (NRSV). Downpours in streambeds in the ancient Near East could bring destructive flooding, while water in a wasteland where no humans lived seems to be a waste of a precious resource. These images, however, are of one who has extra resources and is willing to spend them in places beyond the greatest need. Through God's questions to Job in vv. 25–27, we are reminded along with Job that God's resources are beyond compare.

This reminder is in line with another comment made in this section. God says to Job in verse 21, "Surely you know, for you were already born! You have lived so many years!" (NIV). This was said in apparent affirmation of Job's knowledge of all the things God was asking about. To be sure, this line could certainly be read in a sarcastic tone, and God may have been speaking ironically. However, it might be possible to hear in this a reminder that human days are limited in number. As such, our remembrance of God's dominion can also be limited. Perhaps God's questions of Job were driving at something deeper than humiliation.

A clue may be found in verses 22–24, where God said to Job, "Have you entered storehouses of the snow, or have you seen the storehouses of the hail, which I have reserved for the time of trouble, for the day of battle and war? What is the way to the place where the light is distributed, or where the east wind is scattered upon the earth?" (NRSV). These verses appear odd, even for this cosmic whirlwind tour. Why should Job know about snow storehouses or where hail is housed? Even more odd is the idea that God has hail stored up for a day of battle and war. The clue to all of this may be the light and the east wind that scatters over the earth.

The east wind is referenced in various texts in the Old Testament. In Genesis 41, Pharaoh described a dream in which a scorching east wind dried up seven ears of grain. The interpretation of this aspect of the dream was that there would be seven years of famine in the land. In Hosea 13, the prophet proclaimed that God would send an east wind to destroy the works of the northern kingdom. However, in other texts, such as Psalm 48, God used the east wind to save Israel. Most famously, twice in Exodus—in chapters 10 and 14—Moses stretched out his hand, and an east wind came to his aid. First, in chapter 10 Moses raised his staff, and an east wind brought locusts on the land of Egypt. Then, in chapter 14 an east wind helped split the sea so the Israelites could cross on dry ground.

Therefore, when we read of the east wind that is stored away it may be important to remember that we are being reminded not only of God's dominion over the cosmos but also of the tools God uses for the mighty, saving acts of God's people. What all this may point toward is a God whose dominion extends throughout the cosmos, whose creativity and extravagance in bringing about order in creation are broader than we often imagine, and whose questions to Job were intended not to humiliate or "put him in his place" but, rather, to remind him of his own limitations so he could remember God's saving ways.

Job 38:39–39:30

Beginning in 38:39 and continuing through all of chapter 39, the attention of God's questions turned to the animal kingdom. God opened by asking Job about his ability to provide food for lions, ravens, and their young (38:39–41). The questions again suggest that Job was unable to accomplish something that God is able to do. However, the next examples do not follow this pattern. Instead, many of them fall into the pattern of describing animals that do things that are paradoxical. For example, the mountain goats and the deer give birth after an unknown set of months, only to see their young grow up and leave them (39:1–4). In essence, they labor intensively and produce offspring who know nothing of their mothers' pain.

Later, wild donkeys, animals of burden, are freed from their ropes (v. 5). One would expect them to rejoice at this. What happens instead, however, is that the donkeys run away and live in a wasteland as a mockery of those who stress themselves out back in town (vv. 6–8). Is this a good thing for them to do? It is not clear. For some, being free from work and stress would be beneficial. However, living in a wasteland and having to search for food every day would bring stress in its own way. The paradox of the example should not be lost.

Perhaps the oddest example offered is the ostrich, portrayed as one who lays eggs and then leaves them in the sand, unmindful of the dangers lurking about them (vv. 13–18). Verses 17–18 suggest that God did not create the ostrich with enough wisdom to care about danger. God's comments here could be interpreted as something less than caring; however, the fact that ostriches continue to survive and that God gave them enough speed to outrun horses suggests that, again, we are supposed to see a paradox.

There is another reversal of fortunes in verses 19–30. First, the horse, which was just outrun by the ostrich, is highlighted as one of the mightiest of God's creations, charging into battle without fear (vv. 21–23). Then the entire tour of the animal kingdom ends with a vision of the hawk and eagle, flying high about the earth (vv. 26–27). From there they are able to detect food and feed their young ones upon the blood of the slain (vv. 29–30). These slain were perhaps the slain from the battle in which the horse was charging.

What are we to make of these paradoxes Job is asked about? Perhaps more than simply showing Job oddities of creation or yet again reminding him of the limits of his knowledge, these paradoxes show the multitudinous ways that God's created order is more complex than the theological framework with which Job and his friends were working in the dialogues. Perhaps their simple idea that suffering is due to sin while good things are bestowed on those whom God loves was not a sufficient explanation of the way things actually work.

Job 40:1–15

Chapter 40 begins with God answering Job anew and asking what Job's response would be to what was shared. Job's answer was important. In verse 4, Job said, "I am of little value, what can I return to you? My hand I place over my mouth." This response could be interpreted as a value statement about Job and, by extension, humanity. As such, it would be a way of highlighting the great gulf between humans and the divine. While this is certainly justified, I am not convinced that this is all we should understand Job to be saying. To be sure, the previous exchange highlighted God's dominion and the paradoxes of creation. God showed Job the places he could not go and the paradoxes he surely did not fully understand. However, it may be that Job realized now that, even though he spoke correctly about himself, he still had something to learn. Instead of seeing Job as stating his unimportance, perhaps we should recognize that he was simply acknowledging the difference between himself and God and was willing to listen to the next part of God's speech.

Job 40:6–14

From this point, the speech repeats the pattern from the beginning of chapter 38. In verses 6–14, God implored Job to prepare himself to answer in much the same way the speeches from the storm began. One of the important points made in this introductory section is that Job was not like a god. In verses 10–14, God invited Job to put on majesty and glory, to pour out his anger, and to tread down the wicked. This invitation, which Job could obviously not perform, could be read as a form of taunting, as if God were saying, "You surely cannot do this like I can!" However, in line with Job's response and the paradox of creation, perhaps this was yet another reminder that humans were not meant to do certain things, and one of those things humans were not meant to do was to remove the wicked from the world. This would certainly be important in light of Job and his friends' arguments about who got to stand before God. If Job and his friends were arguing about whether God would acknowledge the wicked, perhaps this statement from God was a reminder that God's dominion did not work according to their rules. Thus, with a repetition of the invitation to answer, God's speech began its final argument.

Job 40:15–41:34

The final section of God's speech was divided into two parts. In each section God focused on a mythical creature under God's care. The first, described in 40:15–24, was Behemoth, an ambiguous animal that has been compared to a hippopotamus or some other primeval monster. The strong creature was described as one of the "first of the great acts of God" and a being who could only be approached by its maker (v. 19, NRSV). The second creature was the Leviathan, a mythical monster often associated with chaos. This beast was described in great detail and, by its description, looked something like a crocodile (41:12–24). It could not be captured, and even the gods of the ancient world were afraid of it (v. 9). The monster lurked amidst darkness yet breathed fire and destroyed anyone who attempts to tackle it (vv. 19–21, 26–29).

Yet, amidst this awesome display of fire and brimstone—certainly meant to overwhelm Job, and us as readers—we are left with a reminder that God's dominion extends even to these places. While these two creatures are terrifying and overwhelming, not unlike the experiences Job endured, there is no place that God's dominion does not extend. As such, Job was reminded at the end of God's speeches that nothing Job endured was beyond God's dominion. However, Job was also reminded that creation was not nearly as simple nor as tame as he may have previously thought.

Within God's dominion are extreme paradoxes and untamed creatures of incredible chaos. What this offered Job was not necessarily a portrait of comfort. God's presence in the midst of suffering may be part of the picture from God's speech. However, one has to also accept that God's creation and the order of it is far beyond any simple explanation of cause and effect or control and divine will. The speeches from the whirlwind leave us at a place where we must simply acknowledge God and the reality of paradox in creation. This acknowledgment leads to the end of the book of Job, where our reading of God's love in the Old Testament can best be summarized.

Job 42:1–9

Chapter 42 begins with Job's answer to God after the whole of God's speech from the whirlwind. The answer lasted six verses and brought to the forefront a number of significant issues. First, Job admitted again that God was in a different category than creation, saying, "I know that you can do all things, and that no purpose of yours can be thwarted" (v. 2, NRSV). Interestingly, Job admitted to what he knew after being asked this very question repeatedly by God. In fact, in verse 3, Job quoted back God's initial question, "Who is this that hides counsel without knowledge?" (38:2; 42:3, NRSV). Job finally decided to answer God's questions.

Job acknowledged that God was able to do anything and that no purpose of God's is thwarted. While the translation offered by the NRSV is acceptable, the phrase "no purpose of yours is thwarted" might better be read as "a purpose or discretion will not be withheld from you." The Hebrew word translated as "purpose" is a rare word in the Old Testament. In fact, it is only used five other times. Each time it is connected with some form of wisdom. In Psalms 21:11 and 139:20, people plan "wicked purposes" against others. Then in Proverbs 1:4, 2:11, and 3:21, the word is used to refer to something that must be taught to the young who are considered naïve or in need of instruction in wisdom. What this might alert us to is the nature of the rest of Job's response to follow. He was not simply admitting that God is all-powerful, as the English translations make it seem. He was also acknowledging, in good wisdom fashion, that he was in a posture of learning, ready to receive the type of discretion and knowledge evident in God's speeches.

Following his quotation of God's own words, Job said, "I reported and I did not understand; things too wonderful for me and I did not know" (42:3). The verse has important divisions, the pause coming after Job said, "I did not understand." Job began by admitting that he spoke during the dialogues but did not understand what he said. Then the second half of the verse is beautifully poetic. The phrase "things too wonderful for me" serves double duty in the verse—it serves as the end of the first half ("I did not understand things too wonderful for me"), and it begins the second half ("things too wonderful for me I did not know"). In the middle of this, Job came to the place of wisdom, which is the acknowledgment that one must be humble enough to admit one has something to learn. In the dialogues, both Job and his friends were entirely convinced of their arguments. They went round and round their various points for thirty-six chapters, never convincing each other. After two sections of lengthy speeches from God, Job was ready to admit he might have something to learn.

From here, in verse 4, Job again repeated part of God's speech before adding his own words in verse 5: "I had heard of you by the hearing of the ear, but now my eye sees you" (NRSV). Recall, the fact that God showed up to respond to Job's request for a meeting with the divine was not to be taken lightly. Here, Job acknowledged that God's engagement was no small thing. While Job admitted he did not fully understand what he had been saying, he also admitted that his encounter with God brought about something transformative for his understanding.

Then Job said a set of words that have confounded interpreters significantly. The Hebrew literally reads something like, "Therefore, I reject and I [comfort, console, change] upon dry dust and ash" (v. 6). Most translations render the verse as a form of Job's repentance. However, as some interpreters have pointed out, read in the larger context of what happened, one might ask of what Job has to repent.[1] Remember, Job was blameless, upright, fearful of God, and shunning evil. Some people point to pride as Job's sin, but we have not seen that to be the case. Job humbly admitted that he spoke of things he did not know, and he acknowledged the difference between himself and God.

Similarly, Job went on to say, "I reject," but what, precisely, did he reject? One other place where this verb is used in a similar grammatical fashion is Job 7:16. In this verse, Job said, "I reject," and most translations supply "my life" based on context in the rest of the verse. Perhaps in chapter 42 the thing Job was rejecting now was not his life but his understanding of what it meant to be human in light of God's presentation about God's dominion and the paradoxes of creation. Remember that part of Job and his friends' arguments were predicated on the framework that humans had a predictable

1. See David J. A. Clines, *Job 38-42*, *Word Biblical Commentary* 18B (Nashville: Thomas Nelson, 2011), 1218–23; J. Gerald Janzen, *Job*, *Interpretation* (Louisville: Westminster John Knox Press, 1985); Ellen F. Davis, *Opening Israel's Scriptures* (New York: Oxford, 2019), 348–59.

relationship with the divine. It was a framework of relationship with God in which humans must be blameless, upright, fearful of God, and shunning of evil in order to avoid suffering. Perhaps Job came to reject that way of understanding.

If so, how do we make sense of the latter half of verse 6? Part of the reason most translations and interpretations present verse 6 as a statement of repentance is that, in the ancient Near East, dust and ash had an association with mourning and repentance. In Jonah, for instance, when the king of Nineveh heard the word of God, he called for a fast that included putting on sackcloth and sitting in ashes (see Jonah 3:6). These types of practices were often linked with mourning and outward penitence. However, ash and dust appeared earlier in Job. In the opening narrative section, Job sat on a pile of ash in a time of deep anguish as he picked at the boils he had been infected with after all his other losses (2:8). Later, Job told his friends that their proverbs were made of ashes and clay (13:12). Finally, in 30:19, Job said of God, "He has cast me into the mire, and I have become like dust and ashes" (NRSV). This last instance highlights that in the book of Job, dust and ashes can be understood as a way of referring to the things of this earth that make up what it means to be human.

What if what Job was doing in his second response to God was not necessarily repenting in the sense that most Protestants think of—confessing some sin or wrongdoing? What if, instead, Job was rejecting a previous way of thinking about what he thought it meant to be human or how to relate to God? This interpretation would also make some sense of the other verb in the second half of verse 6, often translated "console." In a number of examples with this verb and the Hebrew preposition that follows it, the phrase is rendered "change one's mind about." For example, in Exodus 32:12, Moses argued with God about God's plan to destroy Israel after bringing them out of Egypt. Moses said, "change your mind and do not bring disaster on your people" (NRSV). Likewise, in Jeremiah 18:8, the prophet proclaimed God's word to Israel, saying, "if that nation . . . turns from its evil, I will change my mind about the disaster that I intended to bring on it" (NRSV). These texts highlight that the verb is most commonly associated with a change of direction about something, often God changing God's determination for judgment in light of human response. In Job, however, Job was changing his own mind about the way he understood his relationship to God.

If this is the case, however, what other proof do we have to support such a reading of this notoriously difficult Hebrew poetry? The book does not end with Job's response to God. The rest of chapter 42 is a return to a narrative portion of text. In it, God chastised Job's friends, saying, "My wrath is kindled against you . . . for you have not spoken of me what is right, as my servant Job has" (v. 7, NRSV). If God was referring to the last thing Job said, then Job spoke correctly about: 1) his rejection of his previous understanding of the way things work in God's creative order; 2) his rejection of the way he and his friends argued about rightness before God and the nature of suffering; and 3) his willingness to welcome a new understanding that is based on awe and paradox. This would seem plausible, given that God was upset with Job's friends for what they said of God (v. 7) and because God required Job to offer sacrifices for the three friends in order for God's anger to be quieted (v. 8).

Job 42:10–17

By the end of the book, Job received everything back twofold and lived to an old age (vv. 10–17). Such a conclusion is often reviewed poorly by readers of Job primarily because many believe the book is about theodicy—the question about God and the problem of evil—and they feel that Job getting everything back undercuts the message. Some feel that Job getting everything back lets the God of chapters 1 and 2 off the hook for the suffering Job endured. Others feel that Job should not have gotten anything back because Job was prideful and should have been happy just to be alive. Both extremes miss the point of what happened at the end of the narrative.

If one reads carefully, one first notices that Job did offer sacrifices for his friends but not for his family. If you remember back to the first chapters of Job, one of the things Job regularly did to maintain his blameless and upright relationship with God was make regular sacrifices for his children after their feasts (1:4–5). In the end, Job offered no sacrifices when the family gathered. Second, the fact that the text explicitly states that Job named his daughters and gave them each an inheritance (42:15) was especially extravagant and unusual within its ancient Near Eastern cultural setting. These things highlight a different Job than we've yet seen. Now, instead of arguing with his friends, Job was performing sacrifices for them so they could avoid God's anger. Job did not seem to worry much about what would happen as a result of sharing meals with friends and family. Instead, it seems Job was willing to entertain others in his own home and offer a place of hospitality so people could enjoy a place of extravagance so great that he named his daughters and gave them an inheritance.

Conclusion

At the end of the book, Job appears to have learned something about what it means to be human and live well before God in light of the encounter he had. Perhaps the most important lesson he learned was that he could not control everything in his world, nor could he completely understand it. Many of us want control—not necessarily such total control as to live a life without God but a type of control like Job and his friends sought throughout the book. At first, Job tried to control his world through being blameless, upright, fearing God, and shunning evil. He practiced regular sacrifices, even on behalf of his children. He was the type of person who worked diligently to keep everything at bay and in its proper place.

Then suffering happened. In the narrative, it occurred because God was proud of Job as one of God's best servants. In our lives, suffering occurs for reasons we certainly cannot fully know. In my life, my dad got cancer and died. I had tried really hard to be perfect so that things like that would not happen. I was super spiritual growing up. I found my identity in going to church, participating in youth group, leading Bible studies, answering the call to ministry, and many other things. None of it kept me from suffering.

For some, that result would point to reasons not to believe in God. I certainly understand some of the arguments I have heard from people who have suffered greatly and unjustly. However, one of the places where I found the love of God in the Old Testament was when I read Job and realized it was not primarily about explaining why suffering occurred but about how God might be present in the midst of chaos, paradox, and creation. I had often thought about the love of God in very romantic ways. I sang plenty of songs that had me convinced God felt a certain way about me. I have no doubt there is truth to that image of God's love too. However, in the midst of my grief over the loss of my dad that made no sense to me, God's showing up to Job and showing him the paradox of the cosmos while inviting Job to respond offered me hope. Job's rejection of some old ways of thinking and entering into new ways of being also offered me a new understanding of what it meant to be in relationship with a God of love.

Questions for Discussion

1. In what ways do you find yourself trying to control your life? How do you respond when things go out of your control?
2. Why follow God if doing so does not protect us from suffering and grief?
3. How can the Christian community console the grieving among us without erring like Job's friends with their well-meaning but inappropriately applied theology? What are practical ways of showing up in which we can share God's love with the grieving, rather than trying to make sense out of the incomprehensible?

Bibliography

Clines, David J. A. *Job 38–42. Word Biblical Commentary* 18B. Nashville: Thomas Nelson, 2011.

Davis, Ellen F. *Opening Israel's Scriptures*. New York: Oxford, 2019.

Janzen, J. Gerald. *Job. Interpretation*. Louisville: Westminster John Knox Press, 1985.

9. THE TENDER-LOVING MERCIES OF GOD

PSALMS

MICHAEL G. VANZANT

Hear my cry, O God; listen to my prayer.
—Psalm 61:1

Show us your unfailing love, LORD, and grant us your salvation.
—Psalm 85:7

THE EMOTIONAL, HEARTFELT CRIES of the psalmists echo through the hearts of humans through all generations. Images of despair, suffering, questioning, and fear flood the pages of the Psalms as Israel sought to understand the unfairness of a broken world. The words resonate with everyone who experiences loss, hate, cruelty, lies, and a multitude of other personal and communal disruptions to *shalom*. Throughout the Old Testament, a threatened hope for *shalom* fills the pages with imagery of barrenness, famine, and grumbling unfaithfulness. The prophet Jeremiah described a people in such a state: "'Peace, peace,' they say, when there is no peace" (6:14). When will peace come? When will comfort and hope return to a broken world? Humanity toils, manipulates, fights, screams, and strives to find *shalom* with fists raised to heaven, crying, "How long, O God?"

"Peace (*shalom*) to you" is a greeting that encompasses the purpose and meaning of life in the Old Testament. *Shalom* is the idea of elusive peace in an often brutal world. The meaning of the Hebrew word *shalom* is so vast that one word—or even ten words—cannot fully embrace its essence. The picturesque Hebrew language provides broad strokes of the beauty and scope of living *shalom*. Translated numerous ways that attempt to grasp its particular meaning for each specific situation in the biblical text, the depth of meaning of *shalom* becomes lost in the English language. Translations that include the words "prosperity," "health," "wholeness," "completeness," "goodness," "well-being," and "peace" are in themselves inadequate descriptors for the complex yet simple word *shalom*. Complex in particulars yet simple in purpose, *shalom* reflects the image of God's will for all creation. In fact, to understand this word, we must start with creation.

Shalom echoes in the very act of creation as God spoke into the chaos and darkness to bring order. The very essence of an earth that was in its beginning "a formless void" (Genesis 1:2, NRSV) reflected a distressing lack of wholeness and completeness. Creation was then called "good" (*tov*) as the orderly process unfolded daily before the reader. The final day ended with the creation of humans in God's own image. On that day, God proclaimed that it was very good! *Shalom* is tied closely in meaning to the Hebrew word for "good," *tov*. The Hebrew term does not connote a modest evaluation, such as in English usage with good, better, and best. *Tov*, rather, is total completion—all that is right in God's creation. After this proclamation of ultimate goodness, God rested, like a great artist or composer who realizes that the work is complete and nothing more needs added. Creation was whole, complete, and at peace with God in the beauty of God's goodness.

The story of brokenness through rebellion, pride, and self-serving behavior cracked the goodness of *shalom*. The search for *shalom* throughout Israel's history revealed the people seeking peace in blessings but on human terms. It is as if, reflective of their broken perspective of *shalom*, they fixated on Deuteronomy 28 to the exclusion of the rest of God's vision for them in the Torah. In Deuteronomy 28, the people were told that if they were obedient, God would bless them; if they disobeyed, they would be cursed. In the heart of biblical *shalom* blessing, however, is always the divine presence—God with us. Yet throughout their biblical history, many in Israel focused instead on the blessing of all the good "things" of life. Blessing, in Israel's thoughts, became crops, children, wealth, military victory, security, protective nationalism, and a religious system that ensured that God would bless them. Israel's critiques of its own kings in the Old Testament were often that they sought peace through human means (see 1 Samuel 8; Isaiah 30:1–5). Eventually the possession of much wealth, property, and power became their evidence of blessing. The search for *shalom* in the good "things" of life failed miserably through judgment and loss of all that had become Israel's security. The cries of the psalmists often reflected the lack of justice in a broken and *shalom*-less society: "How long will you defend the unjust and show partiality to the wicked? Defend the weak and the fatherless; uphold the cause of the poor and the oppressed. Rescue the weak and the needy; deliver them from the hand of the wicked" (Psalm 82:2–4, NIV).

The enemy growls; the future is bleak; the end is near. The following psalm continues in the same vein: "O God, do not remain silent; do not turn a deaf ear, do not stand aloof, O God" (83:1, NIV). These images encapsulate the struggles of multiple generations as injustice, ungodliness, and despair fill the world with brokenness. It is easy to see the enemy crouching at the door (Genesis 4:7). Surely, the Lord will return soon! Yet, within the weeping and groans of the psalms, hope comes through remembrance of God's mighty deeds. The faithfulness and mercy of God in the past give hope for the future: "I will sing of the LORD's great love forever; with my mouth I will make your faithfulness known through all generations. I will declare that your love stands firm forever, that you have established your faithfulness in heaven itself" (89:1–2, NIV).

The psalmists suggested that the presence of a faithful, loving God was the essence of *shalom*. Still, they questioned where they were to find *shalom* and whether there was hope for *shalom* amidst their circumstances. Once again, the depth of Hebrew connectivity leads to another rich and powerful Hebrew word, *hesed*, the tender-loving mercy of God. *Hesed* is the love that will never give up. *Hesed* is different from the common Hebrew word for love (*ahav*). *Hesed* is mercy made fresh every morning. *Hesed* is the cry of God to return to God, and it is the Torah's call to love God and love others.

Shalom is not about personal welfare but divine good for all humankind. *Shalom* is not *shalom* if it is only for personal comfort. Thus, the prophets demanded a return to proper relationships rather than focus only on religious practices. *Hesed* cries out to us to come back to completeness in relationship and to return to covenant faithfulness to God and one another. *Hesed* is that endless, lavish love of God like the farmer who flings the seed of salvation everywhere, regardless of the soil's worth by human standards (Matthew 13). *Hesed* calls for reconciliation, restoration, and resuscitation of sincere faith. God cries out for covenant restoration, reiterating the notion, "I am your God, and you are my people!"[1]

God's willingness to pay the price for the return of *shalom* is obvious in the messianic prophecy of Isaiah's Suffering Servant. The Servant—bruised, beaten, and bleeding—"was pierced for our transgressions, he was crushed for our iniquities; the punishment that brought us peace [*shalom*] was on him, and by his wounds we are healed" (53:5). Yet Isaiah also envisioned a day when *shalom* would once again fill creation with goodness. The One would come who would proclaim good news to the poor, freedom for the captives, and release from darkness for the prisoners (Isaiah 61:1; Luke 4:18). The wolf will feed with the lamb; the child will play by the viper's nest and not be bitten (Isaiah 11:6–9; 65:25). All are images of wholeness in creation and the fulfillment of *shalom*—the goodness of God's will established once again. My, what a day that will be!

In the meantime, we live in this day. Humanity can neither live in the past nor dwell in the comfort of the future. Still, the tender-loving mercy of God is present and visible within those who live in trust. God's faithfulness and love flow through the pages of the biblical text as all of creation groans for restoration to completeness, wholeness, and peace. God calls us to live in *shalom*, in peace, in this life with God. In this period of the already/not yet of living between Christ's first coming and future return, God still calls us to love God and love others—to be agents of *shalom*. The acts and rituals, superficiality of faith, and the responsibility of life are issues that face believers

1. See, for example, God's speech to Israel in Isaiah 43.

in a broken world. The prophet Micah clarified God's desire for a *shalom*-giving life:

> With what shall I come before the LORD and bow down before the exalted God? Shall I come before him with burnt offerings, with calves a year old? Will the LORD be pleased with thousands of rams, with ten thousand rivers of olive oil? Shall I offer my firstborn for my transgression, the fruit of my body for the sin of my soul? He has shown you, O mortal, what is good. And what does the LORD require of you? To act justly and to love mercy and to walk humbly with your God.
>
> (Micah 6:6–8, NIV)

In God's goodness of *shalom*, in the completeness and wholeness of *shalom*, and in the call to *shalom* relationship with God and others, God proclaims that our superficial faith and religious activity will not restore brokenness. Our going through the motions will not bring *shalom*. Nor will our attempts to defend from the enemy our faith, our rituals, or our way of life given to us. Between verse 7 and verse 8 in Micah 6 is perceived a potent pause where God whispers, "*No—*shalom *is richer, incredibly more beautiful, and the only healing for brokenness.*"

In the beauty of creation, in never-ending *hesed* of mercy and love, God has shown us what is "good" in the Hebrew sense. This goodness found in the *shalom* of creation defines the answer to the question, "What must I do?" Do justice. View the world through the eyes of God, seeing every human as a creation of God who is valued and was loved to the point of death on a cross. Embrace the mercies of God that avail hope and *shalom*, and then recklessly spread it upon all people, regardless of the value the world places on them. Ultimately, accomplishing these things is possible only by walking humbly in the embrace of God's presence. We are dependent, humble, needy, and broken humans redeemed in goodness and grace. Humility—or faith like a child—is a characteristic of *shalom*. Immanuel—"God with us"—is not just a song we sing at Christmas. It is the reality of a God with is, in us, and empowering us to bring the wholeness craved by all of creation.

The Psalms

Throughout the centuries, the psalms have served the community in corporate worship and personal devotion. The characteristics of psalms as prayer, praise, and a call to faith reveals the human need to relate to one who is greater than us, revealed through God's own will through human history. It is a mystery of life that God hears the cries of humanity bound in misery—including that of our own making—and saves.[2] Understanding the images of God's love in the psalms begins the untangling of mystery and the healing of misery. James Luther Mays reveals the complexity of the psalms within a complex world: "Psalms is a virtual compendium of themes and topics found within the rest of the Old Testament. The marvelous works of God in creation, judgment, and salvation, Israel's story, the law of life . . . the majesty and tragedy of the human condition, the everlasting and present kingdom of God—all belong to the agenda of the psalms."[3]

Psalms as a collection of poetic literature is different from other literary genres in Scripture. The emotive nature of the psalms reveals not only God's word for us but also our word to, and about, God. Interpreting Psalms begins with the human perspective within poetry. Words have life in themselves and contain the breath of the speaker. In Psalms we see human life in a broken world. Readers should embrace and breathe the emotions and feelings of each author's work. The psalms reveal enemies, pain, sorrow, and fear. The psalmists display their faith through their questioning, even as they long for God to act decisively.

---

2. Within the Bible, this includes misery that humans bring upon one another as well as misery we individually bring upon ourselves (see Exodus 3:7).

3. James Luther Mays, *Psalms*, *Interpretation* (Louisville: Westminster John Knox Press, 1994), 1–2.

Given that all of Old Testament literature is covenant-driven, the psalms require us to read them through the lens of covenant. The promise of God to be with Israel wherever their journey took them, if they kept the covenant agreement established in the Torah, filters through the psalms in both joy and fear, pain and release. "Do not forget" was the cry of the people to God and from God to the people, as if to say both, "Remember us" and, "Remember what God has done." As such, the psalms reveal an unexpected twist to worship. Questioning implies faith in one who can do something about the situation. Because of this, Israel's covenant songs (psalms) remain a vital part of the human experience in worship.

The psalmists portrayed a deep understanding of the dissonance of the transcendent God who spoke creation into existence and the immanent God who entered into the muck of life, bringing hope and a future. *Shalom* is a gift God offers to a broken world through the goodness of God's own tender-loving mercies. God alone saves God's people with the expectation that they will fulfill God's promise to Abraham at his call, "and in you all the families of the earth shall be blessed" (Genesis 12:3, NRSV). All of creation resounds with praise for God's goodness and the completeness offered through God's tender-loving mercy.

Psalm 103:1–5

A diligent study of the psalms should be a lifelong endeavor and is impossible in a short period of time and space. Psalm 103, however, is an excellent example of the declaration of hope in a broken world. Psalm 103 begins (and ends) with a call to join in praise to the Lord of *shalom*-giving *hesed*. "Praise the Lord, my soul; all my inmost being, praise his holy name. Praise the Lord, my soul, and forget not all his benefits—who forgives all your sins and heals all your diseases, who redeems your life from the pit and crowns you with love and compassion, who satisfies your desires with good things so that your youth is renewed like the eagle's" (vv. 1–5, NIV). Verses

1 and 2 begin with the Hebrew word *barakhi*, "Bless!" The idea of blessing requires presence. *Barakhi* carries the human responsibility of full attention to the blessed one. The term means to kneel in awe and wonder of God's holy goodness and *shalom*.

Shalom begins with praise from the human's center of being (see v. 1). The psalmist eschewed an outward sacrifice as an act of praise, instead looking inward. Change of perspective begins in the midst of our gut-felt fear, anger, and despair.[4] God desires us, not our works, duty, or motions. Verses 1–2 may be paraphrased, "In all that I am, I will praise and bless you, my Lord. From the depths of my being, from the darkest places in my soul I will call upon your mercies! Bless the Lord, O my being, and forget not all of God's dealings with God's people, and the benefits God has provided in the Torah covenant."

Remember who is able to forgive and heal. Remember the great God of Genesis 1, who came into the mud to bring life in Genesis 2. This One who reaches into the pit of despair and *shalom*-less existence is the One who freely wreathes us in *hesed:* tender-loving mercy and deep-felt love for the one in despair and lost in sin. Remember God with us, who called us into a covenant of community with God. Remember the words of God to Abraham, Moses, Joshua, and all of us: "I will be with you wherever you go." Remember the mercies of the God who *is* the God who sees, hears, cares, and delivers Israel from slavery and is still seeing, hearing, caring, and delivering the brokenhearted and providing *shalom* to the distressed.

Remember and do not forget the God who does not only give material blessings that we take for granted, such as air, food, and water but is also the God who has shown us goodness in creation. God satisfies, fills, and completes our desire for *shalom*. The "good things" of verse 5 can be translated as being clothed or decked out with goodness. Youthful joy and transparent faith are renewed like the

---

4. In Hebrew thought, decisions involved the "bowels," where the impact of decision-making is felt.

eagle's as God's mercy brings rebirth and a taste of creation goodness filled with the dreams and hopes common to young people whose lives lie before them, ready to soar from the nest.

The opening section of Psalm 103 addresses the first question with which every human must wrestle to find an answer. What is, and how do we relate to, that which is bigger than us? In the ancient context of Psalm 103, no doubt is found concerning the existence of a god. Every people group worshiped something. The realization of a greater power and interaction with that power took several directions. Many ancient cultures developed systems of faith and worship that they assumed would control or manipulate their god. If they brought sacrifices, followed laws, and quoted formulas of faith, their god would bless them with grain, children, and wealth. Israel fell into this trap of manipulation and found that acts of religion were worthless without restoring covenantal relationships. God spoke through Amos, saying, "I hate, I despise your religious festivals; your assemblies are a stench to me!" (5:21, NIV). Encountering God's love in its fullness will satisfy our need for goodness and renew us through God's tender-loving mercy.

Psalm 103:6

"The LORD works righteousness and justice for all the oppressed" (NIV). God's never-ending, tender-loving mercy has a task—a burden—to accomplish in and through us. The goodness of creation ended with everything right, normal, and just. Everything was in balance and at rest. This balance is the essence of righteousness in Hebrew. Righteousness was the norm in creation. All was right in the world. *Shalom* filled the lungs of all breathing creatures and bathed the oceans, plants, and trees with beautiful sunlight. The innocence of creation *shalom* was shattered when sin entered the world. The brokenness of the world grew quickly in biblical accounts. God's chosen people were called to be lights of *shalom* to the world as blessings to all nations (see Isaiah 42:6). Yet, even in their freedom from the oppressive yoke of slavery in Egypt, their brokenness took them into the oppression of idolatry and sin. The eighth-century-BCE prophet Amos revealed the societal issues that broken *shalom* brought to the chosen people. Throughout Amos's prophetic text, we see this brokenness in his description of Israel's sin, crushing the heads of the poor and selling them for a pair of sandals (Amos 2:7–8). "You lie on your ivory couches, you dine on choice meats until you are stuffed, you drink wine by the bowlful and use the finest ointments" (6:4, 6a). In response to these *shalom*-breaking hypocrisies, Amos thundered: "But let justice roll on like a river, righteousness like a never-failing stream!" (5:24, NIV).

The burden God carries and works to correct is righteousness and justice for all people. Only God is able to restore the righteousness and justice of *shalom* within the chosen people. Israel's oppression by the nations who took them into exile had a direct relationship to the oppression of *shalom* in their own society through a lifestyle of worshiping other gods and their belief in the illusion of self-sufficiency. Often Israel's history reveals a nation that was secure in its economy, its military capabilities, and a corrupt king. God's justice and righteousness were part of God's good creation. *Shalom* does not come through human prosperity or power in a broken world. God alone works righteousness and justice in and through us as agents of *shalom* in the world. We are new creations with the opportunity to experience the goodness of God and to take that goodness to creation around us.

Psalm 103:7–12

"He made known his ways to Moses, his deeds to the people of Israel: The Lord is compassionate and gracious, slow to anger, abounding in love. He will not always accuse, nor will he harbor his anger forever; he does not treat us as our sins deserve or repay us according to our iniquities. For as high as the heavens are above the earth, so great is his love for those who fear him; as far as the east is from the west, so far has he removed our transgressions from us" (NIV). Verse 7 calls us to remember God's dealings with Moses. Remember that God met Moses on the mountain. Remember the God who provided the way of life and relationship with the God of *shalom*. Remember the great deeds of God through the salvation history of Scripture. Consider the blessings of divine presence in Israel's history. God has revealed his goodness to us through deeds of redemption and salvation. Once we remember, we discover many important aspects of God's grace, mercy, and kindness.

The LORD is filled with compassion for all creation and the people of the earth (v. 8). God views every soul with passion and affection. Compassion describes a tenderness and softness, as a parent with a newborn. The joy of hearing the cry of a newborn baby and realizing the total dependence this little one is experiencing moves our hearts to tenderness. When humans understand our dependence, rather than demanding our independence, we can experience the merciful compassion of God with us. Compassion describes the motive, if not the nature, of the *hesed* love of God.

God's love revealed in graciousness describes more than unmerited favor to those who do not deserve it (vv. 9–12). The purest and simplest expression of grace is presence. God's grace is God with us. In the sins of his people, God still comes and delivers. God is filled and abounding with *hesed*-love and mercy: slow to anger and quick to forgive. God's gracious compassion is not "fair" in human terms, concerning our sin. Fairness requires punishment for our sin; someone must pay for the damage done. Fairness demands an eye for an eye, a tooth for a tooth. The wages of sin is death. Apart from God, no life is possible. Israel discovered this fact through exile when they refused God's mercy and did not return to their Creator. Evil will consume evil without divine intervention. God's everlasting love is offered to all who will turn back to this gracious presence. God's *hesed* is renewed every morning (see Lamentations 3:22–23). Incredibly, God desires to forgive humans, even seeking us out through the prophets of old and through the Holy Spirit today. God's mercy does not repay evil with evil but with love, grace, and mercy.

Therefore, the psalmist proclaims in verses 11–12, "For as high as the heavens are above the earth, so great is his love [*hesed*] for those who fear him; as far as the east is from the west, so far has he removed our transgressions from us" (NIV). Fearing God carries the meaning of standing in awe of One who could crush us for our sins yet embraces those who stand dependent on God's presence. Imagine a child standing before a parent, caught red-handed, all the facts known, and expecting nothing less than a harsh admonishment. However, as the child's tears flow in sorrow and repentance, the loving parent embraces the little one, holding them close, and simply says, "Go and sin no more." The matter is never mentioned again. All is as it was.

The powerful proclamation of forgiveness for those who stand in awe before a gracious Savior in verses 10–12 defines the result of *hesed*-driven *shalom* for humankind. Romans 8:1 reveals Paul's inspired view of God's mercy on the cross: "Therefore, there is now no condemnation for those who are in Christ Jesus" (NIV). Yet this powerful image of divine love and mercy in the book of Psalms discloses a loving God with outstretched arms hundreds of years before the cross. Abounding in *hesed*, God is that parent filled with love and mercy for a repentant child, whose very heart desires *shalom* for creation.

Psalm 103:13–18

God's compassion like a father, passion for the broken one, and knowledge of our frailty drive the purpose of the psalmist in exclaiming the need for humanity to experience the tender-loving mercy of God. The brevity of life is on the minds of humans continually as loved ones die and the reflection in the mirror ages. Yet in the ancient world, violence and destruction were a way of life. Death was a constant reminder. Comfort in knowing that God "knows" (v. 14) enhances our appreciation for God's mercy and presence. God made us from dust (v. 14; see also Genesis 2:7). Whenever the wind blows dust into our eyes, we are reminded once again of our frailty and dependence. Whether one is a millionaire or a custodian of others' property, all becomes dust in the end (see Genesis 3:19). Life is a wisp of smoke that soon is no more. In Hebrew thought, we see an image of one cut off from the land of the living (Psalm 103:15–16). When a parent died, their memory lived on through the next generation. Those who died with no offspring were considered truly dead, soon to be forgotten. The winds blow, and the nameless millions are remembered no more. This bleak picture of human destiny described the crisis of Godless, *shalom*-less people. Mortals' desire for fame and a name for themselves will die with them regardless of human accomplishments. The winds of time will erode names off monuments of honor and pride.

Still, there is hope. This section of the psalm ends with inconceivable hope for insignificant humans: "But from everlasting to everlasting, the LORD's love [*hesed*] is with those fear him, and his righteousness with their children's children" (v. 17, NIV). Forever, for eternity, God's mercies will prevail in human lives through all generations. The rightness and justice of *shalom* is still possible, on one condition: keeping covenant. Covenant is an agreement between two parties that provides "benefits" (v. 2, NIV) for those who keep it. This covenant is different from any made between humans. This covenant is from a being who needed nothing from us, nor could we offer anything that would make God more complete. At first glance, it seems to be a covenant that is too good to be true. God simply says, "I will be your God, and you will be my people." Yet a holy God making a covenant with unholy humans required stipulations of holiness in us. "Be holy because I, the LORD your God, am holy" (Leviticus 19:2, NIV). The commands and precepts provided to Israel were not hoops to jump through or checklists to mark off each day to make God happy. The price of *shalom* was remembering to obey God's principles of life.

The Torah provided the path to relationship *shalom* between the people and God and within the community itself. Loving God and loving others is revealed in the structure of the Ten Commandments and repeated explicitly in Leviticus 19:18 and Deuteronomy 6:5, *and* Jesus combined these two commands to describe the greatest instructions of the Torah (see Matthew 22:37–38). In so doing, Jesus connected the two statements as a united whole, defining the only path to *shalom* or salvation: love God; love others. All of the laws and precepts correlated to maintaining *shalom* between God and humans and humans and humans.

Loving God is the primary stipulation for covenant. Loving with whole heart, whole soul, and whole strength is a picture of the totality of being. Furthermore, all of life was within the covenant with God. Living with the *shalom* of God's tender-loving mercy in the center of community was critical. God's people should live in unity and tender-loving mercy with one another, living by the law. The law required doing justice, loving mercy, and walking humbly with God. When seen through the Abrahamic promise and Levitical law, Israel's place as God's chosen agents of shalom *required* blessing to all the families of the earth.

Psalm 103:19

"The LORD has established his throne in heaven, and his kingdom rules over all" (NIV). God's throne in heaven declares the sovereign, transcendent God before whom the people stand in awe (or fear). This verse portrays a great hope for all humankind. The King's covenant is not limited to Israel! The King's domain is not with a single group. From the heavenly throne room, the King rules over *all* people. God's dominion is all of creation. The image of the ideal king revealed in Scripture is one of benevolence, protection, and compassion. The king weeps over the souls lost in battle. The king provides in time of famine and want. The king is a servant to the people whose power is used for the welfare—*shalom*—of the community. The King on the heavenly throne is not bloodthirsty or self-serving. The King's dominion is just, righteous, and only requires humility and trust in the King's goodness and mercy.

For Israel, this verse offered a different kingship model than that of a human king in a specific geographic location. The heart of God's kingdom was not limited to the temple of Jerusalem. We see the presence of the transcendent God who spoke creation *shalom* into existence—a God whose realm dwarfed the gods of the world of ancient Israel. Each nation around Israel worshiped a god who was theirs alone, who sat within a temple made with human hands, and, most of all, was a god imaged by human hands. Israel's interpretation of Torah throughout their monarchy led to the mistaken idea that Jerusalem would not fall because God lived within the temple.[5] Israel's history portrays that *shalom* cannot be found in protecting one's place as God's chosen nation or people. The temple was destroyed by the Babylonians, rebuilt after exile, and destroyed again by the Romans in the first century AD. Israel's journey through Scripture, leading into the era of the New Testament, describes a people who wanted kingdom restored on earth, where their rightful place as the chosen people was made evident. Yet God's kingdom is over all people. The dual nature of God's transcendence and intimacy equates to a God of all people. God's *hesed* of tender love and mercy is a gift for all who come in repentance. *Shalom* is offered to the entire kingdom of God: peace on earth to all humankind.

Psalm 103:20–22

"Praise the LORD, you his angels, you mighty ones who do his bidding, who obey his word. Praise the LORD, all his heavenly hosts, you his servants who do his will. Praise the LORD, all his works everywhere in his dominion. Praise the LORD, my soul" (NIV). This

5. Such a belief is countered within the Old Testament itself in the narrative that immediately precedes the people's cries for a human king (see 1 Samuel 4).

final section of the psalm calls all of creation to active worship: Bless the Lord! Bless the Lord! Bless the Lord! Bless the Lord! The fourfold ending of the psalm embraces everything that humanity cannot see but must trust. Praise the Lord all the messengers (angels) who do as required in obedience to the King, mighty ones created by God, who represent God's unending work to bring *shalom* to creation (v. 20). Praise the Lord all the heavenly hosts who do the will of God (v. 21). The stars and planets join the heavenly realm in praise to the One who set them in order to be light in the darkness (v. 22). They fulfill their purpose as a symbol of God's creation *shalom*—completeness and order. Praise the Lord, everything! For nothing exists apart from God's will and command. God's work holds the universe in order. Even as stars, comets, and meteors move and fall, the order of creation continues. The universe itself embraces the changes of time just as seen on earth. God's *hesed* is at work in constant care and attention. Praise the Lord, my soul!

The fourfold conclusion brings all of creation—from the four corners of the world to the far reaches of space—together to celebrate the completeness of God's work, the goodness of God's gracious presence, and the beauty of God's tender loving mercies that forgive our sins and restore our souls for *shalom* in us and for others. Humans are but a speck in the greatness of the universe and a dot across the course of eternity. Yet the King of the universe came down with healing in his wings.

Conclusion

Understanding the covenant relationship between God and the people chosen by God aids in encountering the love of God in the Old Testament. The issue of God's sovereignty as the almighty Lord and the obvious responsibility of Israel to follow the covenant willingly reveals the complexity of the story. The psalms reveal the paradox of human free will and divine holiness. Yet this paradox is a critical part of the creation story revealed in God's transcendent and immanent nature. How many times has the Sunday school teacher heard the question, "Why did God plant the tree in the first place?" While the issue is complicated, the truth is found in the image of God as love. The very concept of love in a holistic sense requires free will. Relationship built on love requires risk and acceptance that pain may result. No one can *make* anyone love. In the Old Testament story of God's interaction with creation, God provided every opportunity for humans to love as God loved, as seen within the act of creation itself.

God reveals true love in God's character, revealed throughout salvation history. Human terms for loving others are in stark contrast to God's never-ending love. The prophet Hosea declared God's weariness of the fickleness of human love: "What can I do with you, Ephraim? What can I do with you, Judah? Your love is like the morning mist, like the early dew that disappears" (Hosea 6:4, NIV). The psalms reveal with clarity the differing characteristics of God's love and human love in a fallen world. Broken humanity demands certain others meet stipulations before love is given. God loves unconditionally. The stipulations are not conditions for God to love humans. The stipulations are that humans love God also. Through reciprocal love, humanity may experience the love offered through the very being of God.

In today's terms, God's *hesed* love is all-in love that is determined to love regardless of response. The biblical text reveals the lengths to which God goes to show this love and to provide every opportunity for humanity to know it. Still, the psalms show us that God will not override free will. God's *hesed* will never end, but it must be accepted, embraced, and acted out in life. One who knows mercy must show mercy. One who knows divine love must share divine love with all people but especially with the least of these. *Hesed* wrapped in the Torah and the great commandment of Jesus to love the Lord your God with all your being and love your neighbor as yourself is a way of life. Jesus's command echoes Micah 6:8, "He has shown you, O people, what is good [complete, whole], and what does the LORD require of us? But to do justice, love *hesed*, and walk humbly with your God." In Old Testament terms, love requires love, mercy requires mercy, and presence requires presence. All-in love requires an all-in response.

Questions for Discussion

1. What psalm draws you near to God when you are in a place of despair? What do you hope to find in that psalm when you read it?
2. As you read Psalm 103 again, make a list of the ways God has fulfilled verses 2–5. What are areas you might be struggling with today that need God's compassion and love to overcome?
3. What would you share about God's tender-loving mercies from Psalms with those who are unchurched or with a believer struggling with a crisis in life?

Bibliography

Mays, James Luther. *Psalms. Interpretation.* Louisville: Westminster John Knox Press, 1994.

10. EXILE AND THE GOD OF LOVE

ISAIAH 43:1–7

BRAD E. KELLE

THE STATE OF CALIFORNIA, where I live and teach, has an official state song called "I Love You, California." The lyrics move sequentially through the various things that the songwriter treasures about the state, particularly elements of nature (redwood forests, Golden Sierras, and the "grand old ocean"). But the song especially expresses the deep sense of attachment the songwriter feels to California with the words, "You have won this heart of mine."

In a volume like this one, where we are exploring Old Testament texts that reveal God as a God of love, Isaiah 43:1–7 is a special case. It has all the forthrightness of California's state song as God declares—explicitly, personally, and directly—God's love for Israel. In fact, Isaiah 43:4 is the only verse in the Bible where God actually uses the direct-address phrase "I love you" in speaking to God's people. There are, of course, other Scripture passages that affirm God's love for Israel or hint at this expression through metaphors and images.[1]

Some of these can present problems for contemporary readers. Among the other Old Testament prophets, for example, Hosea used the metaphor of a parent and child to offer a retrospective of Israel's life as the chosen people. Through Hosea God declared, "When Israel was a child, I loved him, and out of Egypt I called my son" (Hosea 11:1, NRSV). Zephaniah emphasized God's love for Israel in a proclamation of future restoration: "The LORD, your God, is in your midst . . . he will renew you in his love; he will exult over you with loud singing as on a day of festival" (Zephaniah 3:17, NRSV). The book of Malachi, set in the difficult time after the exile, when the people struggled to reconstitute the Jewish community in Jerusalem, opened with God's response to the people's accusation that God did not love them—a response that included a past-tense version of the

1. Outside of the prophetic books, see, for example, Exodus 34:6; Deuteronomy 7:7–8; and numerous psalms that proclaim God's "steadfast love" for the people that "endures forever" (e.g., Psalm 136).

statement of God's love in our passage in Isaiah: "I have loved you, says the Lord" (Malachi 1:2, NRSV). Jeremiah's proclamation of comfort to the earlier generation of exiles in Babylon (a passage with several similarities to Isaiah 43:1–7) came the closest to God's direct statement of love in Isaiah 43:4, although it was still a statement about the past: "I have loved you with an everlasting love; therefore I have continued my faithfulness to you" (Jeremiah 31:3, NRSV).

As these examples show, no other passage proclaims God's love for God's people in the direct, personal, and present-tense way we find in Isaiah 43:1–7. God's "I love you" in verse 4 stands apart as the most explicit, first-person declaration of God's love in all of Scripture. Even John 3:16, commonly seen as the Bible's quintessential proclamation of God's love, offers only a third-party description ("for God so loved the world") and not the direct, divine pronouncement found in Isaiah. God's declaration of love in Isaiah 43 is especially emphatic because it appears alongside statements about how much God values the people—"you are precious in my sight, and honored" (v. 4, NRSV); and within a larger context that speaks of Israel as God's own special possession—"I have called you by name, you are mine" (v. 1, NRSV); "everyone who is called by my name, whom I created for my glory, whom I formed and made" (v. 7, NRSV).

The forthrightness of God's declaration of love in Isaiah 43:4 is surely noteworthy. But the power and significance of the divine "I love you" comes fully into view when we read it within its context. The prophet's announcement of God's love in Isaiah 43:1–7 came to God's people at a death moment, a null point—a time of when they found themselves living in exile, feeling they had squandered their special identity and lost their sense of belonging. Into that moment of disruption, disconnection, and disorientation, God spoke a word of love that would make a new future possible.

The Context: Exile, Judgment, and Loss

Isaiah 43:1–7 was a promise of deliverance, return, and restoration from God through the words of an ancient prophet to those Israelites living in exile in Babylon long after the destruction of Jerusalem in 586 BCE. It stands as the first of four units that make up chapter 43 (see vv. 8–15, 16–21, 22–28), and provides an opening oracle of salvation—an announcement that the Israelites were about to be saved from their captivity in Babylon and given a new future back in their promised land. In verses 1–7, however, we find a marked emphasis on helping the people overcome a sense of lost identity and abandonment in order to move into a new future. The prophet's message named Israel as a people who belonged to God from their beginning and to whom God had a deep sense of attachment—"you are mine" and "called by my name" (vv. 1, 7, NRSV).

The historical context of the middle part of the book of Isaiah (chapters 40–55) is the aftermath of destruction and exile. In the early years of the sixth century BCE, the Babylonian empire exerted imperial dominance over the lands in and around the kingdom of Judah. Eventually, a series of conflicts, rebellions, and invasions resulted in the capture and destruction of Jerusalem by the Babylonians and a sequence of forced deportations of people from Judah to live in exile in Babylon (see 2 Kings 24–25). In the assessment of most contemporary interpreters, the middle section of Isaiah addressed an audience that had lived in exile in Babylon for a long time—perhaps nearly fifty years. Many had experienced firsthand the destruction of Jerusalem, the death of loved ones, and the traumatic experience of being forcibly driven thousands of miles from home to live in a foreign country. Others among the audience of Isaiah 43:1–7 had likely been born and raised in Babylon, learning from an early age the traumatic memories of death and destruction in the past and knowing only the realities of life as a colonized group trying to make their way in Babylonian society and culture. For many in this community, the memory of life in the land of Judah was distant at best;

and the thought of returning home to live in their land of promise likely seemed unrealistic—if not arduous, dangerous, impossible, and perhaps even unwelcome. No wonder our passage refers to the journey home from Babylon as one marked by difficulties described metaphorically as passing through waters, rivers, and fire (v. 3).

By the time of the prophetic announcement in 43:1–7, however, something had changed. The Babylonian empire was fading, soon to be replaced by the Persian empire under Cyrus the Great, who would eventually declare that exiled peoples like those from Judah could return home and reestablish their lives back in their places of origin (see 2 Chronicles 36:22–23; Ezra 1:1–4; Isaiah 44:28; 45:1). In that context, the God of Israel announced a new word of restoration: the time of judgment associated with the exile had ended, and now God would deliver the people from Babylon and lead them home to Jerusalem. In the book of Isaiah, chapter 40 marked this new moment, even as it marked a new section of the book that turned from primarily proclamations of judgment and exile (chapters 1–39) to announcements of redemption into a new future (chapters 40–55). The well-known declaration in Isaiah 40:1–5 opened the second section of the book by proclaiming comfort to Jerusalem, declaring that the time of judgment had ended, and envisioning a way through the wilderness that would lead the exiles home. A new moment, in which God would do a new thing for the exiles, had dawned. Just two chapters later, Isaiah 43:1–7 provided a detailed oracle of salvation that grounded this new beginning for the Judean exiles in God's love for the people.

Alongside this historical background, the immediate literary context of Isaiah 43:1–7 sheds additional light on this new declaration of God's love and redemption for the exiles. The preceding passage in Isaiah 42:18–25 was a prophetic message chastising Israel for being "deaf" and "blind" (vv. 18–19, NRSV) and for failing to understand God's works and fulfill the role of being God's people in the world. Israel was called to be God's "servant" (v. 19, NRSV) who would open the eyes of others and lead them to God, but Israel itself failed to observe and understand God's ways.[2] Portions of this passage give important insight into the experiences and suffering of the exiles that God would address in Isaiah 43:1–7.

For instance, 42:22 described the exiles as a people who were "robbed and plundered" by others and had become trapped as in "prisons" and vulnerable like "prey" being hunted with no one to rescue them (NRSV). But the passage is dominated by the people's voice and perspective. Their assessment of the situation of exile and the reasons for it was entirely negative, with no sense of new possibilities. In the people's perspective, the destruction, suffering, and exile they experienced were God's judgment for their sin. Even so, the violent actions of judgment described here were not God's intentions and were not part of God's nature (see v. 21); they were called forth as a response to disobedience within God's covenant relationship with God's people. The people's own first-person words in verses 24–25 declared that they sinned by rejecting obedience and for that reason God's anger manifested itself as judgment. And this is the note on which chapter 42 ended. The final words of the oracle described images of God's hot anger and a burning fire.

Seen against this literary context, chapter 43 introduced a sudden and dramatic new word that shifted from the people's focus on what happened and why, to God's focus on who Israel still was as God's people and how they could receive a renewed future. Isaiah 43 changed the focus from Israel's past disobedience and judgment to God's present word of loving assurance, which opened the possibility for a new future. As Brevard Childs notes, only when we consider the "full judgmental dimension" of what has come before can we clearly

---

2. Dorothy Kelley Patterson and Rhonda Harrington Kelley, eds., *Women's Evangelical Commentary: Old Testament* (Nashville: Holman Reference, 2011), 1214.

see the "full force of the extended grace" that God offered through the prophet's message in chapter 43.[3]

The Divine Promise: Belonging, Deliverance, and Restoration

Given the content of the immediately preceding passage and the shift in tone and perspective introduced in 43:1–7, the NRSV's translation of the opening Hebrew word of Isaiah 43:1 is apt: "But now." With that disjunctive phrase, the prophet began to proclaim a divine promise of salvation for the people ("thus says the LORD") that reversed the course of judgment and failure and provided three different assurances to the exiles (vv. 1–2, vv. 3–4, vv. 5–7). In a context of destruction, loss, and exile, the first and last assurances both began with God's encouraging command to the people: "Do not fear" (vv. 1, 5, NRSV). Perhaps even more fittingly for a context in which the exiles felt they had lost their sense of identity and belonging, the passage as a whole began and ended with the same keywords ("created," "formed," "called"—see vv. 1, 7, NRSV)—a reassurance that the people belonged to God from the beginning as God's own creation and that the original bond was not broken by their sin or the dire consequences that came from it.

The opening part of verse 1 began the passage's first assurance (vv. 1–2) with the prophet introducing the message God would speak directly in the second half of the verse. Here the proclamation that the exiles were those whom God "created" and "formed" was on the lips of the prophet (NRSV). This proclamation introduced the first of two main themes that featured throughout the divine promise of restoration from exile in 43:1–7—namely, the theme of God's loving claim of possession over a people who felt abandoned and without identity. Along with the language of creation and formation,

3. Brevard S. Childs, *Isaiah*, Old Testament Library (Louisville: Westminster John Knox Press, 2000), 334.

the opening of verse 1 reinforced God's claim over the exiles by referring to the people as "Jacob." This reference drew the hearers back to Israel's special calling and election that began with Abraham and Sarah in Genesis 12 and continued through God's covenanting with their ancestors, such as Jacob and his family. The exiles' identity as God's chosen, covenant people—called by God to participate in the divine purposes in the world—remained in place. Although the passage would soon turn to imagery drawn from Israel's exodus from Egypt, God's promise of deliverance and restoration was grounded first and foremost in the "signal act by which Israel came into being—namely, God's electing of the offspring of Abraham"—and that was an act that exile did not undo.[4]

When God began to speak directly in the second half of verse 1, God's first words to the exiles facing an uncertain future were, "Do not fear." This phrase was a classic formula used in salvation messages throughout the Old Testament prophets and occurring often in Isaiah 40–55 (e.g., 41:10, 13, 14; 44:1). In this verse, however, the admonition not to fear found its grounding and reason in another assertion—this time by God in the first person—that the exiles belonged to God as God's special possession. God's words in the second half of verse 1 echoed those of the prophet in the verse's first part but with an emphasis on the special, divine choosing of Israel ("I have called you by name") and, perhaps more strikingly, on God's own feeling of attachment to the people ("you are mine"). Overall, the opening verse of this message to the exiles made it clear that God took the initiative to bring Israel into being and had not relinquished that initiative. The possibilities of a return from exile and a new future that would be described in the verses to come existed solely because of God's creative and redeeming actions taken toward God's

4. Christopher R. Seitz, "The Book of Isaiah 40–66" in *The New Interpreter's Bible*, vol. 6 (Nashville: Abingdon Press, 2001), 375.

people, and the grace-filled, passionate attachment to them felt within God's heart.

Verse 2 completed the first divine assurance to the exiles by explicitly introducing the second of the two main themes that featured throughout the promise of restoration in 43:1–7—namely, the theme of Israel's exodus from Egypt (see Exodus 13–14). In this verse, God declared complete divine protection for the exiles during their journey home with language and imagery that evoked God's initial and decisive act of deliverance from slavery. The various prophetic messages across Isaiah 40–55 often portrayed the return from exile as a second exodus that would once again lead the people out of captivity and reconstitute them as a distinct people belonging to God (e.g., Isaiah 44:27; 50:2). Here, however, the imagery went beyond that of the original exodus story, envisioning a journey not just through waters but also through rivers, fire, and flame. Images of burning may appear here because they were used elsewhere in Isaiah as symbols of divine judgment (e.g., 1:25, 31; 6:13). Whether through obstacles from the outside or the effects of judgment brought on by the people's sinful past, God promised divine presence and protection with the same words offered to Moses at the burning bush: "I will be with you" (v. 2, NRSV; see Exodus 3:12).[5]

Verses 3–4 constitute the second divine assurance to the exiles. These verses continued to use the imagery of the exodus for God's rescue of the exiles but also reiterated even more emphatically that the people's hope for deliverance was grounded in God's deep attachment to and love for them. The opening divine declaration in verse 3 ("I am the LORD your God") echoed the prologue to the first commandment (Exodus 20:2) given at Sinai just after the exodus from Egypt. The rest of the verse also evoked the memory of God as Israel's redeemer in the events of the first exodus by referring to giv-

5. The precise Hebrew words in Exodus 3:12 and Isaiah 43:2 differ, but the meanings correspond exactly.

ing Egypt over for the sake of Israel's freedom. Now, however, God was turning a past deliverance into a present promise. As in verse 2, the declaration in verse 3 went beyond the elements of the original exodus story, with God promising to give Ethiopia and Seba, alongside Egypt, as a ransom payment to accomplish Israel's deliverance from their Babylonian masters. Ethiopia (also known as Cush, or Nubia) was the land south of Egypt, and Seba was likely a region in or near Ethiopia. Neither of these two nations figured into the exodus story, but the biblical tradition linked them together with Egypt (see Genesis 10), and the text seemed to use all three nations together as a reference to the entirety of Africa (see also Isaiah 45:14). The dramatic message was clear: God was willing to pay a steep price in order to free Israel from Babylonian exile.

The language used in verse 3 that described God giving over certain kingdoms for the sake of Israel's liberation from exile sounds like sheer favoritism for Israel at the expense of others and may be troubling for contemporary readers. Are we to conclude that God exchanged these kingdoms for Israel because God valued them less? The latter part of verse 4 adds to the potentially troubling image, since God made an even more general-sounding determination to exchange other "people" and "nations" for Israel's return (NRSV). Interpreters often look to history to solve the dilemma presented by verses 3–4, linking them with the military activity of the Persian emperor Cyrus—God's chosen deliverer for the Babylonian exiles according to the book of Isaiah (see 44:28; 45:1)—as he took control away from Babylon in the years leading up to 539 BCE. Seen in this way, the text indicated that God would grant Cyrus dominion over Africa, to Israel's benefit and as part of Israel's redemption—a notion mentioned explicitly in the context of a description of Cyrus in Isaiah 45:14.

But perhaps a more symbolic interpretation of these verses and the nations named within them is in order and better explains the troubling passage. After all, Egypt, Ethiopia, and Seba were relatively minor players in the events of Persia's rise and the end of Israel's exile. Perhaps we are better off seeing these nations as symbols for those forces that have acted in hostility toward Israel and brought about a share of their suffering. Perhaps we should understand Egypt, Ethiopia, and Seba as representatives of Israel's robbers and plunderers described in Isaiah 42:22. Seen in this way, verses 3–4 follow the Old Testament principle of corresponding punishment (an eye for an eye, see Exodus 21:22–25). The prophet announced that, in order to accomplish Israel's rescue, God would bring about a reversal of status: those who plundered Israel would themselves become the spoil of other hostile powers, while Israel stepped out of all the violence and into a new future of peace and restoration. As another possibility, perhaps verses 3–4 reflected the context of ancient Israelite civil law that required the payment of a high price in order to compensate for the loss of a victim (see Exodus 21:30).[6] Seen in this way, God offered other nations (including Egypt, Ethiopia, and Seba) not as an indication that they had less value than Israel but precisely because they possessed the kind of worth that marked the redemption payments mandated in Israel's laws.

In any case, sandwiched between God's declarations of exchanges and ransoms was the definitive statement of the reason for these divine actions—the most explicit and poignant declaration yet of God's deep attachment to and passionate affection for God's people: "Because you are precious in my sight, and honored, and I love you" (Isaiah 43:4, NRSV). As noted already, this statement bore similarities to Jeremiah 31:3–10, in which God declared God's love for Israel in the context of a promise to gather the exiles home from various parts of the earth. As also mentioned previously, although the Bible often speaks of God's love for Israel, nowhere was it expressed as directly and powerfully as in the concise statement of Isaiah 43:4. Exiles who may have felt abandoned, lost, or worthless heard that God loved and cherished them. In the context of the full salvation

6. Childs, *Isaiah*, 334.

oracle in 43:1–7, this unabashed divine declaration of love anchored the entire promise of restoration in the single motivating factor of God's love for God's people.

This divine declaration was even more powerful when compared to the way that "love" language was used in royal inscriptions from kingdoms around the wider world of ancient Israel.[7] Royal inscriptions from places such as Assyria and Egypt frequently described gods expressing their love for the king, but here God proclaimed God's love for the entire people of Israel. The presence of love terminology in ancient pacts and treaties also reminds us that the word "love" here expressed more than just feelings of affection. It denoted the loyalty that was meant to exist between covenant partners. To love was to show loyalty. Just as other Old Testament texts called Israel to express their love for God as loyalty and obedience (see Deuteronomy 6:5), the description of God's actions on Israel's behalf given in verses 3–4 showed God's loyalty to God's people, even when they had not previously shown loyalty to God (see Isaiah 42:18–25).

Verses 5-7 comprised the final divine assurance given to the exiles. In verses 5–6, God moved from the proclamation of the motivating factor of divine love to the most explicit and detailed description of the return from exile itself. As with the first assurance (vv. 1–2), this final assurance began with God's comforting command, "Do not fear" (v. 5, NRSV). In verse 1, the reason not to fear was "for I have redeemed you" (NRSV)—a general statement about the exiles' status and identity that fit with the passage's opening focus on a people created, formed, and called by God. In verse 5, following the description of God's protection and provision for the journey home given in verses 2–4, the reason not to fear was aptly stated as "for I am with you" (NRSV). What followed was a statement of God's intention to gather the scattered people of Israel from all directions of the earth.

---

7. Shalom Paul, *Isaiah 40-66: Translation and Commentary* (Grand Rapids: Eerdmans, 2012), 207.

While the language used here ("east . . . west . . . north . . . south . . . end of the earth," NRSV) employed a figure of speech to refer to the entirety of the known world, at the time of this prophecy, exiles from Israel were indeed widely scattered throughout nations such as Assyria, Babylonia, Egypt, and more. God's promised redemption was comprehensive.

Perhaps most significantly for a situation marked by experiences of displacement, dispersion, and loss of identity, however, God's declaration of the re-gathering of the exiles in verses 5–6 used family language. God linked together the exiles scattered in different parts of the world by calling them "offspring" (literally, "seed" or "kin") of one another (v. 5, NRSV), reestablishing a sense of belonging and identity as a people. God also named those displaced and dispersed as "my sons" and "my daughters" (v. 6, NRSV). These designations reflected the language used to express the covenant relationship between God and Israel elsewhere in the Old Testament ("Israel is my firstborn son," Exodus 4:22; Hosea 11:1, NRSV), and its use here reaffirmed that special parent-child relationship for the exiles. The language in Isaiah even expanded the typical covenant formula, going beyond gender restrictions with an inclusiveness not to be missed as God announced that sons *and* daughters constituted this special family and would be restored together (v. 6; see also Joel 2:28). Even those exiles who had been scattered far from their home, away from the temple and promised land that represented their connection to their God, remained part of a special kinship with God as their loving parent.

This theme of identity and belonging continued into the final verse of the passage. At the close of God's proclamation of restoration for the exiles, verse 7 returned to the opening announcement to the people in verse 1 so that the passage began and ended on the same note. Once more, the verse named the exiles as those who had been "called," "created," and "formed" by God (NRSV). At the end of God's declaration, however, what began as an address to Jacob/Israel (v. 1) is now applied to all members of God's people scattered in every area around the world. Moreover, there was a new emphasis in this final divine proclamation that further explained the exiles' identity as God's people and God's reason for acting to rescue and restore them. God emphasized that the exiles were called, created, and formed "for my glory." The Hebrew of verse 7 placed "for my glory" at the center of the verse as *the* reason that God brought Israel into being. While the Hebrew word order of verse 7 made this emphasis clear, it did not make for smoothly readable English. A more literal translation of verse 7 would read, "All those who are called by my name, and *for my glory* I created them, I formed them, and, indeed, I made them."

When read in this way, the passage's final statement in verse 7 emphasized that Israel was created originally for the purpose of glorifying God in the world, and the exiles were being restored so they could return to that initial divine calling. This conclusion connected to some of the key Old Testament passages that defined Israel's identity from the beginning as a people called for the sake of the whole world and elected for the purposes of carrying God's redemptive presence to all people as priests (see Genesis 12:1–3; Exodus 19:5–6). But the language of glorifying God as part of a mission to the world had even more resonance within the immediate context of Isaiah 40–55. These prophetic oracles wrestled with the realities of destruction and exile and tried to understand what those experiences meant for Israel as those called by God to reach all peoples. In so doing, the prophetic messages in exile actually reconfigured Israel's long-standing mission and identity within the Old Testament.

For example, some texts in Isaiah 40–55 spoke of Israel's role—even in the midst of the experience of destruction and dispersion—as a "light to the nations" (e.g., Isaiah 42:6; 49:6). Many of these references occurred in the so-called Servant Songs (42:1–4; 49:1–6; 50:4–9; 52:13–53:12), which described a servant appointed by God to administer justice (good judgment and just treatment) in the context of exile, not only among God's people but also to all nations. In later Christian tradition, interpreters read these poems as referring to Jesus, yet the only text that gave an identity for the servant identified him as "Israel" (the collective people; see 49:3). Several other passages in Isaiah also spoke of Israel (or Jacob) as God's chosen servant (e.g., 41:8–9; 44:1–2, 21; 45:4; 48:20). Even if more precise identities were intended, the Servant figure symbolized the role Israel was called to fulfill within God's larger work to redeem all nations—and it was a role to be performed right in the midst of exile. Taken together, various passages in Isaiah 40–55 announced the surprising divine word that the exile would actually become the vehicle by which Israel could carry out its original calling to be an instrument of blessing and a priestly kingdom to all the world. These prophetic words insisted that the exile did not cancel or even delay the covenant people's task of being the instrument to bring the life-giving blessing and knowledge of God to the nations. No, in a most unexpected way, they proclaimed that the job of carrying God's presence to the nations remained even in the midst of exile.

The final words of Isaiah 43:1–7 tied into the larger prophetic message about the exile with God's assertion that Israel was originally created and was being reformed specially "for my glory" (v. 7, NRSV). Several of the passages throughout Isaiah 40–55 that described God's servant or the larger divine mission in which the exiles could participate referred to God's glory being made known. To be a "light to the nations" and to participate in bringing God's redemptive presence to the world was to make God's glory known among all people. In Isaiah 42:8, for instance, God declared that the divine glory had been given to Israel—even in exile—so they might help the nations see that glory (see also 49:3). In the final words of Isaiah 43:1–7, God likewise reminded those exiles who had lost their sense of identity, belonging, and purpose that they remained created, formed, and made to glorify God. Why was this the case? Isaiah 43 gives one reason: God loved them.

The Message: Ongoing Love

In a volume of essays exploring portrayals of God's love in the Old Testament, Isaiah 43:1–7 stands out for several reasons. The most apparent is that verse 4 contains a direct and poignant statement of God's love for God's people unmatched by any other passage in Scripture. But a deeper significance emerges when we place that divine declaration of love into the context of this passage as a whole. God's "I love you" stands structurally at the center of the passage and thematically at its heart. Isaiah 43 presents God's love as the motivation for all of God's promises to the exiles and all of God's acts of redemption and restoration. Out of God's loving attachment to God's people, hope emerged for a new future. In the exile, God's people lost much of their identity and sense of belonging, perhaps feeling abandonment and despair. In response, God's words through the prophet promised not only a return from exile in which God would guide them safely through the dangers (v. 2) but also a renewed sense of being valued, loved, and even created by the God who would restore them. They were not a people without a home or identity; they were the people whom God lovingly claimed as God's own—belonging to God, formed by God, and precious in God's sight (vv. 1, 4, 7). Here is a clear message in Scripture to God's people past and present—especially those who have suffered trauma, loss, abandonment, displacement, oppression, or marginalization. God values who you are. You have an honored place in a special relationship with God, who sees you as beloved and precious. And no experience of loss, hurt, or even failure can invalidate that reality.

Another element of how God's love manifested itself for the exiles in Isaiah 43:1–7 makes this passage significant for today's readers as well. As the divine promises made to the exiles across verses 2–6 indicate, the loving actions of God described here were not one-time occurrences but ongoing and reliable realities. Especially notable in this regard are the perpetual-sounding promises of presence and protection made in verse 2: "*When[ever]* you pass through the waters, *I will be with you. . . . When[ever]* you walk through fire . . . the flame *shall not consume you*" (NRSV). God's people can expect God's love to issue forth in continuous creating, forming, accompanying, protecting, and restoring acts in the face of any and every challenge to God's rule or the life and mission of God's people. In Isaiah 43:1–7, God's love does not promise the exiles a new creation in which all dangers, threats, and adversity have been removed. Rather, it promises a life in which God's people will meet those realities with God's creating, delivering, and loving presence in their midst.

In the end, though, Isaiah 43:1–7 makes clear that there remained only one reason the exiles received restoration and God's people in every age receive the promise of God's ongoing presence in the midst of adversity. The basis of those realities is not the merit that people earn, the achievements they complete, or the actions they perform. God's promises to God's people are rooted solely in God's utterly unmitigated love (v. 4). In the same way that the song "I Love You, California" provides an example of the deep sense of affection and attachment that appears throughout Isaiah 43:1–7, another song from my childhood—a gospel song—captures the core message of this passage: God promised new life to the exiles not because of their own deeds but simply because of who they were to God. In the song "Because of Whose I Am," the songwriter celebrates receiving God's love with these words:

"[God] said, 'I'm gonna love you'
It's not because of what I am
Not because of what I've done
It's because of whose I am."[8]

To God's people past and present, Isaiah 43:1–7 proclaims who they are—cherished, honored, and precious in the sight of the God who

8. Reba Rambo and Dony McGuire, "Because of Whose I Am," (Bud-John Songs, Inc.; ASCAP and New Spring Publishing, Inc., 1980).

created them, restores them, and still calls them to make God's glory known in the world. Why? One reason: God loves them.

Questions for Discussion

1. What kinds of experiences can lead God's people today to sense a loss of identity, belonging, or purpose in the world, and how does the message of Isaiah 43:1–7 help address those struggles?
2. How might today's believers experience God's presence with them in situations of adversity, as the exiles were promised in their journey home?
3. What is the significance of God's inclusion of exiles from all parts of the world (and both sons and daughters) as part of the children of God who are called to participate in God's redemptive work in the world?

Bibliography

Childs, Brevard S. *Isaiah. Old Testament Library*. Louisville: Westminster John Knox Press, 2000.

Patterson, Dorothy Kelley and Rhonda Harrington Kelley, eds. *Women's Evangelical Commentary: Old Testament*. Nashville: Holman Reference, 2011.

Paul, Shalom. *Isaiah 40-66: Translation and Commentary*. Grand Rapids: Eerdmans, 2012.

Rambo, Reba and Dony McGuire. "Because of Whose I Am." Bud-John Songs, Inc.; ASCAP and New Spring Publishing, Inc., 1980.

Seitz, Christopher R. "The Book of Isaiah 40–66" in *The New Interpreter's Bible*, vol. 6. Nashville: Abingdon, 2001.

11. THE OVERWHELMING LOVE OF GOD

HOSEA 11

THOMAS J. KING

DOES THE OLD TESTAMENT include any passionate expressions of the love of God? As the child of missionaries and ordained ministers, I was continually exposed to Bible teaching at the hands of caring and dedicated pastors, Sunday school teachers, youth ministers, and Bible study leaders. At home each evening, my brothers and I listened to stories from a children's Bible that our parents faithfully read to us before prayer time. These experiences instilled in me the earliest foundations of my love for Scripture. They also initiated a lifelong struggle to understand the great love of God.

Some of those Bible stories, even from the children's Bible, still trouble me today. My brothers and I heard that God destroyed the world with a flood, God opened up the earth to swallow rebellious leaders and sent fire to consume others, God commanded the destruction of entire populations including women and children, and God allowed one of the famous prophets to curse young lads who had mocked the prophet's bald head, with the result that two bears mauled the boys. Such accounts, along with numerous others, have left many of us inside and outside the church with the impression that the God of the Old Testament was angry and violent, in contrast to the loving God of the New Testament, who came in Jesus to sacrifice God's own life on our behalf in order to save us from sin and death, and who taught us to love one another.

Over the years my understanding of the anger and violence attributed to God has become more sophisticated. There are a number of important issues related to how we read the Bible, recognize its ancient contexts, comprehend its theological meanings, and interpret God's intended messages embedded in the literature—all of which influence our understanding of God's love. The purpose of this chapter is not to explain all those troublesome texts. Rather, I want to highlight and examine one particular passage that expresses the passionate love of God that may provide additional perspective for recognizing God's love throughout the Old Testament.

The Setting of Hosea 11

Included among the troublesome passages of the Old Testament are those of the literary prophets. It is popularly held that the writings of the prophets of the Old Testament only communicated judgment, doom, and gloom. The prophets only pointed out Israel's sins and pronounced God's judgment in the form of violence and destruction. They spoke on behalf of an angry God who was intent on punishing sinful and unfaithful people. A more careful reading of the literary prophets, however, reveals that they communicated much more than merely threatening oracles of judgment.

Hosea is included among those identified as the eighth-century BCE prophets (Hosea, Amos, Micah, and Isaiah). The major event concerning which the eighth-century prophets warned the people of Israel and Judah was the devastation and dispersion carried out by the Assyrians (described in 2 Kings 17–18). The eighth-century prophets confronted the people with their sins and pronounced judgment in the form of destruction, which came by means of the nation of Assyria.

While it is true that judgment is a significant theme in the books of the prophets, it is rarely the last word. There is a common pattern in the writings of the Old Testament prophets in which judgment oracles are followed by oracles of salvation and restoration (Isaiah 11:11–16; 12:1–6; Amos 9:11–15; Micah 4:1–10; 7:8–20). The movement from judgment to restoration is often mediated by calls for repentance (Isaiah 1:16–19; Amos 5:4–6, 14–15, 24; Micah 6:8). This pattern suggests that God's desire is not punishment and destruction; rather, God's ultimate concern is for reconciliation and renewal.

The pattern reflecting judgment followed by restoration is evident throughout the book of Hosea. Hosea can be divided into two main sections, each of which contains messages of judgment followed by restoration. The first section is made up of chapters 1–3. This section is distinct from the oracles in the rest of the book because it focuses on Hosea's family as a metaphor for God's relationship to

Israel. Judgment is expressed through the names of Hosea's children (*Jezreel*: "God sows [punishment];" *Lo-ruhamah*: "no compassion;" *Lo-ammi*: "not my people;" 1:2–9), and an unfaithful wife, who represents Israel's unfaithfulness to God (2:2–13). These pronouncements of judgment are turned to restoration as the children's names are changed to terms of acceptance (*Ammi*: "my people;" *Ruhamah*: "compassion;" 1:10–2:1; 2:21–23), and the unfaithful wife is reunited to her husband (2:14–20).

The second section of Hosea is made up of chapters 4–14. This section expresses two units of judgment, each followed by oracles of restoration and renewal. Chapters 4–10 contain oracles of judgment capped by an oracle of restoration in chapter 11. Chapters 12–13 return to an emphasis on judgment, and the book concludes with an oracle of promise and restoration in chapter 14.[1]

This consistent pattern in the Old Testament prophets suggests that the purpose of judgment oracles was not to satisfy some malevolent desire in God for satisfaction derived from punishment and destruction. In contrast, the pattern suggests that the purpose of judgment oracles was to highlight the devastation of sin, drive God's people to repentance, and ultimately lead them to reconciliation. The goal of reconciliation expresses God's desire for restored relationships grounded in love. In this context, the restoration oracle in Hosea 11 provides a moving expression of God's passionate love for the people of Israel.

Images of a Loving Parent (vv. 1–4)

The opening verses of Hosea 11 communicate God's initial love for Israel by means of a parent-child metaphor. The JPS Tanakh translation (Jewish Study Bible) provides a moving rendition of the first line of the chapter, expressing God's affection: "I fell in love with Israel when he was still a child." The rest of verse 1 states that

1. James Luther Mays, *Hosea*, OTL (Philadelphia: Westminster, 1969), 15–16.

God called Israel "out of Egypt," and God referred to Israel as God's "child." The reference to Egypt recalls the great exodus event in which God rescued the Hebrews (children of Jacob/Israel) from slavery in Egypt and brought them to Mount Sinai, where God established a covenant relationship with them. Israel as God's child in the context of the exodus event echoes Exodus 4:22–23, where Moses was directed to tell Pharaoh that Israel was God's child and Pharaoh should let that child go. This designation of Israel as God's child establishes the parent-child metaphor that is expressed throughout the opening verses of Hosea 11 and reinforces the concept of intimacy implicit in an image of parental love.

The image of a child, along with the reference to slavery in Egypt, depicts those who are helpless and weak. It has been suggested that, of all the infants in the animal kingdom, the most helpless and dependent is the human creature. At birth, humans cannot walk, speak, or feed themselves, and they carry little or no survival instincts. Human infants require not only physical care but also the emotional attachment of love. In this context, with an image representing helplessness and need, God initiated a loving relationship with young Israel. Israel had nothing to offer God. An enslaved, infantile nation with few, if any, resources reflecting power, might, or great worth was *called* by God *out of Egypt* for the sake of loving, covenant relationship.

The allusion to the exodus event and the covenant at Sinai carries within it an affirmation that God's love is aimed at all people and was not limited solely to Israel. The focal point of the exodus event is God's call to covenant relationship initially expressed at Mount Sinai in Exodus 19. Central to this call was God's desire to make Israel "a kingdom of priests" (v. 6). The idea that the entire nation was to be made up of priests suggests that their congregation should be made up of all the other nations. This is consistent with God's earlier call to their ancestor Abraham in which God proclaimed to Abraham that "all the families of the earth shall be blessed in you" (Genesis 12:3). These two expressions of covenant purpose communicate God's ultimate intention to provide blessing and care to all the world.

A significant feature of prophetic texts is how they often carry a dual sense of application or fulfillment. The second half of Hosea 11:1 is quoted in Matthew 2:15 in relation to Joseph's flight to Egypt along with Mary and young Jesus in order to escape the threat of Herod. After the death of Herod, the Gospel states that Jesus's return from Egypt fulfilled the words of the prophet, "Out of Egypt I called my son." Clearly for ancient Israel in the eighth century BCE, the message of Hosea was focused on reminding Israel of God's love reaching back to the time of Israel's deliverance from oppression in Egypt when the nation of Israel was in its infancy. As is often the case for the words of the Old Testament prophets, this verse was given a second application in relation to the child of God, Jesus Christ, whose life called out of Egypt would bring even greater fulfillment to the establishment of a kingdom of priests by securing salvation for all who turned to God.

Hosea 11:2 reflects the heartache of every parent whose child has gone astray and rebelled. The translation of this verse can appear confusing. For example, the New American Standard Bible (following the Hebrew text) renders the beginning of this verse as follows: "the more they called them, the more they went from them; they kept sacrificing to the Baals." It is unclear who "they" were, who were calling them, and away from what group they were departing when they kept turning to the Baals. The Septuagint (or LXX, the ancient Greek translation of the Old Testament) renders the first verb and the second object of the verse in first-person speech, which provides a translation that better fits the context: "the more I called them, the more they went from me; they kept sacrificing to the Baals, and offering incense to idols" (NRSV). This verse expressed God's frustration stemming from the apostasy of the children of Israel when they refused to respond to God's call and pursued false gods and idols. It is uncertain whether the term "Baals" refers to local manifestations of the main Canaanite god known as the god of storm and fertility, or whether it refers to Canaanite gods in general. The land of Palestine, where the Israelites settled in the midst of the Canaanites, was dependent on rain for its fertility. Storm and fertility were considered by the Canaanites to be under Baal's power and influence.[2] Israel's "sacrificing to the Baals" reflects turning to Baal for sustenance and nurture as the one who controlled the rains and fertility of the land upon which they depended as an agrarian society.

In the denunciation of Baal, the text proclaims that Israel's God is the one who "fed them" and cared for them (Hosea 11:4). Verses 3–4 heighten the parent-child metaphor as God is depicted in relation to parents teaching toddlers how to walk, holding them in their arms to instill comfort and healing, leading them with love, and bending down to feed them. Such images are commonly held to represent God's care and guidance for Israel through the wilderness period. However, as we anticipate the implied development of the metaphor in verses 5–7, the images may serve to recall God's provision for Israel through the wilderness, nurturing Israel through the turbulent time of the judges, and establishing Israel as the nation became a monarchy.

These tender images might readily awaken our own memories as young children or loving parents. The description may even evoke mothering images for God. Comfort and healing call to mind numerous times my father or mother held a cool rag to my feverish brow late in the night when I was ill as a child. The depictions here portray the experiences of loving parents teaching toddlers how to walk, tossing giggling babies into the air only to land securely in loving arms, and playfully coaxing young mouths to open for solid food. The metaphors call to mind the exhilaration of releasing my own little girls' hands, if only tentatively, as they shuffled to take their first steps. Most poignant is the phrase in verse 4 that is often trans-

---

2. John Day, "Baal (Deity)," *Anchor Bible Dictionary*, 1:547.

lated, "I became to them as one who lifts the yoke from their jaws" (NASB; see also RSV, KJV, NKJV, NET, ESV). The stark contrast of an image related to cattle (yoke) in the midst of the affectionate parent-child metaphor has prompted a more fitting reading that is still consistent with the consonantal text of the Hebrew. The intimate love of God is expressed in the NRSV's translation "I was to them like those who lift infants to their cheeks" (see also NIV, NABRE, CEB). Such wording prompts with heartfelt emotion the memory of lifting my own babies up to my face in order to rub noses as I embraced their miniature frames. These were the types of expressions with which God communicated to ancient Israel an intimate, divine love for God's covenant creatures.

God's Response to Wayward Children (vv. 5-7)

In keeping with the parent-child metaphor, one might describe verses 5–7 as representing the anguish and frustration of a parent who feels they must punish their rebellious teenager. The prophet spoke for God in proclaiming, "Israel shall not return to Egypt, but Assyria will be their king because they refuse to return." Verse 5 has been rendered two ways with regard to the initial clause: "They will *not* return to the land of Egypt" (NASB; see also NKJV, KJV, ESV); or "They *shall* return to the land of Egypt" (NRSV; see also NIV, TNK, RSV, NET). The difference stems from how the first Hebrew term in the phrase is rendered and the larger context of the book of Hosea. The Hebrew text begins with the negative particle *lo'* ("not"), which results in the reading, "they shall *not* return to the land of Egypt." However, some have taken that same term to be the Hebrew homonym *lo* ("to him" or "him"), understanding this to be the object for the end of verse 4 ("I bent down and fed *him*"), with the result that verse 5 begins, "they *shall* return to the land of Egypt" (cf. LXX). This second rendering is supported by other statements in Hosea indicating that Israel would return to Egypt (see 8:13; 9:3).

The first reading is understood to reflect the time when Israel appealed to Egypt for help (2 Kings 17:4), and God's response through Hosea proclaimed that such a return to Egypt for aid would fail, and Assyria would become Israel's oppressor (thus, "they shall *not* return to the land of Egypt"). The second reading suggests that Israel would return to Egypt, perhaps as refugees or figuratively, representing slavery and oppression (ultimately at the hands of both Egypt *and* Assyria).[3] Both renderings reflect a situation of punishment and oppression as a consequence of Israel's turning away from God.

Verse 6 reinforces a picture of devastation with the image of a sword whirling against the cities of Israel and destroying Israel's gate bars and consuming Israelite leaders because of their counsel. The sword (a feminine noun in Hebrew) is the subject of all three verbs (each in the matching feminine singular form): "whirl," "destroy," and "consume"—thus depicting the violence and destruction of warfare. In relation to the second phrase of verse 6, the Hebrew term *bad* may refer to a "part," such as a body part like a limb, or the part of an object such as the bar of a gate or fortress; or it may refer to "idle talk" and boasting such as might be associated with a false prophet.[4] This ambiguity results in the various renderings found in English translations: "will demolish their gate bars" (NASB; see also RSV, NET, ESV); "consume their limbs" (TNK); and "devour their false prophets" (NIV; see also NRSV, NABRE). The punishment depicted by such destruction was in response to Israel's scheming (counsel), which sought deliverance and prosperity by means other than seeking the Lord their God. This reasoning is made explicit in the following verse (v. 7). This section of the passage (vv. 5–7) concludes with the indictment that Israel was "hung up" (Hebrew, *tl'*) on continually turning its back on the Lord. The final phrase presents the

---

3. J. Andrew Dearman, *The Book of Hosea, New International Commentary on the Old Testament* (Grand Rapids: Eerdmans, 2010), 285.

4. Francis Brown, S. R. Driver, and Charles A. Briggs, *A Hebrew and English Lexicon of the Old Testament* (Peabody, MA: Hendrickson, 1996), 94d, 95a.

contradiction that Israel called God one who was "high" (or called to the Most High) yet did not lift up or exalt God. Israelites may have said their God was above all, but their unfaithful actions proclaimed otherwise.

In the context of the ancient Near East, Israel's focus on becoming a kingdom of priests (Exodus 19:6) was disrupted by their apostasy and the threat (or false hope of security) represented by the superpowers of the day, such as Egypt and Assyria. Though God had demonstrated time and again the ability to provide for Israel's well-being, Hosea indicted God's children for turning elsewhere for their provision and assurance. These were life-and-death decisions for ancient Israel. In essence, the prophet was highlighting for Israel the difference between life with God and life without God. For a people who began as an insignificant cluster of tribes enslaved in Egypt and surrounded by the greater powers of the ancient Mediterranean world, life without God might have ultimately led to extinction. The testimony of the sacred history proclaimed that God had always been the one who fought their battles for them (Deuteronomy 3:22). The nation was warned against saying in its heart, "My power and the might of my hand made this wealth for me" (Deuteronomy 8:17). The prophet's message communicated that the rejection of God, in favor of self or others, could only lead to the endangerment of life as depicted by whirling swords and ruin. Hosea proclaimed that, without God, ancient Israel's military aspirations and schemes of alliance or tribute for the sake of self-preservation only led to destruction.

In keeping with the conviction that judgment was intended to drive Israel to repentance, this section of the passage includes a significant wordplay. Verse 5 includes the Hebrew term *shuv*, which carries the basic meaning of "turn back" or "return." In relation to God, it could be used to indicate turning away from God as in apostasy, or turning toward God as in repentance. Verse 5 indicates Israel would or would not "return" (*shuv*) to Egypt (reflecting punishment for apostasy) because they refused to "return" (*shuv*) to

God in repentance. The further description of punishment in verse 6 stems from Israel's persistence in "turning away" (another form of *shuv*) from God (v. 7).[5] The greater literary context of Hosea, the eighth-century prophets, and indeed the Old Testament proclaims that God's desire was for Israel to turn toward God by means of repentance (*shuv*) from their sin and apostasy.

Love Overwhelms Anger (vv. 8–11)

Verse 8 signals a dramatic shift, not only by a change of subject (from punishment to compassion) but also by a change in address. No longer was Israel addressed with third-person references (him, them), but now Israel was addressed in the second person (you). It is also striking that the common call to repentance, which normally preceded God's promises of restoration, does not explicitly appear in this passage. Instead, God dramatically turned toward an expression of deep compassion, almost as if God could not wait through the process of repentance, so eager was God's desire to jump to restoration for Israel: "How can I give *you* up, Ephraim? *How* can I surrender *you*, Israel? How can I make *you* like Admah? *How* can I treat *you* like Zeboiim? My heart is turned over within Me, All My compassions are kindled" (v. 8, NASB; emphasis added to pronouns; interrogative emphasis is in original).

The Old Testament stereotype of God as either stoic or angry is nowhere in sight in this verse. The first-person speech of God expressed a passionate love for Israel that overwhelmed the wrath expressed in the previous section. God was not able to deliver Israel to enemies who would punish and oppress God's child. The pain of such a thought turned back, or changed, God's mind ("My heart is turned over within Me"). It has long been recognized that, for ancient Israel, the heart represented the center of intellect and rational

5. Dearman, *Hosea*, 286.

function, which we today would normally attribute to the mind.[6] Nevertheless, an emotional appeal that we would attribute to the heart was also expressed here: "All My compassions are kindled." The poignant force of this wording is reflected in two other passages that use the same Hebrew verb and a similar Hebrew noun. Genesis 43:30 uses these same Hebrew words to describe Joseph's intense emotion ("deeply stirred," NASB; "deeply moved," NIV; "overcome with affection," NRSV) toward his brothers, which moved him to weep. First Kings 3:26 expresses the pathos of a mother trying to save her child from death using the same terminology.[7] Using similar language, Hosea 11:8 expresses God's love for Israel with an overwhelming passion involving both mind and heart.

This section of the passage implies an internal struggle within God in which some compulsion to punish the wayward child, Israel, was implied; but that concern was overpowered by a love and compassion that could not bear to turn Israel over to such trauma. The divine internal turmoil was further expressed by the rhetorical questions, "How can I make you like Admah? How can I treat you like Zeboiim?" The underlying answer was that God, due to immense love, certainly could not treat Israel like Admah or Zeboiim. These two places are not as familiar to many readers of the Bible as are their counterparts. Admah and Zeboiim are proper nouns referring to cities mentioned only here and in Genesis 10:19; 14:2, 8; and Deuteronomy 29:23. The passages in Genesis associate Admah and Zeboiim with Sodom and Gomorrah, and the text in Deuteronomy explicitly describes Admah and Zeboiim as having been destroyed by God's wrath along with Sodom and Gomorrah. The four cities are understood to have occupied the same valley. Deuteronomy 29:23 identifies the destruction of Sodom, Gomorrah, Admah, and Ze-

6. Hans Walter Wolff, *Anthropology of the Old Testament*, trans. Margaret Kohl (Philadelphia: Fortress, 1974), 46–51.

7. See Francis I. Andersen and David Noel Freedman, *Hosea*, *Anchor Bible Dictionary* 24 (New York: Doubleday, 1980), 589.

boiim as a parallel for the devastation God promises to bring upon Israel when they forsake the covenant and serve and worship other gods (Deuteronomy 29:22–28). Hosea 11:2, 5–7 describes a time in which the warning of Deuteronomy 29 had come to bear and Israel deserved the curses of the covenant (Deuteronomy 29:21) that reflected the overthrow of Admah and Zeboiim. However, the passionate cry expressed in Hosea 11:8–9 declared that God's compassion would prevent such treatment.

This reversal portrays God as refusing to fulfill God's own law delivered to Israel, which stipulated that a stubborn and rebellious son (as Israel was depicted in this chapter) should be stoned to death (Deuteronomy 21:18–21). Instead, "compassion, the tender emotion which parents feel toward the helpless child, grows increasingly strong and displaces wrath (cf. Jer. 31:20)."[8] The opening line of verse 9 explicitly expresses this reversal: "I will not carry out the burning of my anger, I will not return to destroy Ephraim." Once again, the term *shuv* ("turn back," "return") was used—this time to express God's determination not to "return" to the decision to punish Ephraim.

The rest of verse 9 provides what appears to be an authoritative statement expressing God's justification for turning away from wrath. God declared, "For I am God and not a human being, Holy in your midst" (Hosea 11:9b). In contrast to humans, who are prone to express their anger through violence, God determined, "I will not come with rage" (v. 9c). God's being and decision were decreed "holy" in the midst of God's children. This announcement presented a profound image: the Holy One, God, chose to remain "in the midst of" a people who too often expressed themselves in unholy and impure ways. It contributes to the Old Testament foundation for the incarnation in which God through Christ became flesh and moved among and touched even those who were considered sinners

8. Mays, *Hosea*, 157; see also 156.

and impure (Matthew 8:2–3; 9:10–11; Luke 15:1–2). The Holy One's determination to abide in the midst of an impure people constitutes a further expression of the love of God in the Old Testament.

The parent-child metaphor shifts to that of a lion and, finally, to images of birds in verses 10–11. Verse 10 depicts God roaring as a lion, in response to which God's children came trembling. The trembling recalls "the fear of the Lord" that is so foundational in the Old Testament Wisdom Literature (Proverbs 1:7; 9:10; 10:27; 14:26–27; 15:16, 33; 16:6; 19:23; 22:4; 23:17). It was a fear grounded in reverence and respect for great power and authority. The verb for trembling was repeated at the beginning of verse 11 in which the children are now depicted as birds and doves. Verses 10–11 portray God's children returning from various places of dispersion and exile: the west, Egypt, and Assyria.

The need to return presumes that God's children had been dispersed as refugees and exiles as a result of their apostasy—depicting a time when the punishment described in verses 5–7 and rejected in verses 8–9 had taken place after all. The message of Hosea 11 is not that God does away with the consequences of sin but that God, unlike human beings, will not respond out of anger (see v. 9). The consequences of sin were woven into the fabric of creation from the beginning, and God as Creator openly accepted responsibility for that, as expressed throughout the Old Testament. The mentality reflected by the Old Testament writers upheld a high view of the sovereignty and authority of God, which recognized no equal or rival next to God (Exodus 8:10; 9:14; Deuteronomy 4:35, 39; Isaiah 45:5-7, 14, 21-22; 46:9; Joel 2:27). Consequently in the Old Testament, God was blamed (and accepted responsibility) for anything and everything that happened in the world, with the implication that if God did not actually will something, God at least allowed it to occur. This view of God's unparalleled sovereignty contributes to the difficulty in understanding a number of Old Testament passages that depict God in unexpected ways.

For example, consider God's response to sin in the garden of Eden. The Lord proclaimed, "*I* will greatly increase your pains in childbearing" (Genesis 3:16, emphasis added). Clearly the disobedience of the first couple and their response of blaming God, the serpent, and each other (Genesis 3:12–13) introduced brokenness and mistrust into their relationships. As a result, without the caring support and companionship of a spouse, the woman would endure childbirth alone, thereby "greatly increasing" the anguish of an already painful process. Though the couple brought this upon themselves, God took responsibility for their actions by, in effect, taking the blame for the way sin played out. God's speech in Genesis 3:14–19, mistakenly understood as God's prescription to the couple, was actually God's description of the state they brought about through their disobedience and resultant mistrust. This was followed by God's gracious work to correct that state of alienation by means of reconciliation, beginning with Genesis 3:21 and extending throughout the rest of salvation history.

Consider also God's role as portrayed in the book of Job. While Satan was the instrument of affliction against Job (1:12; 2:7), God received the ultimate blame (1:16, 21; 2:9–10). Similarly, God sometimes took responsibility for the hardening of Pharaoh's heart in the account of the plagues in Exodus, even though other times Pharaoh was clearly liable for challenging God and attempting to manipulate circumstances to control outcomes for his own benefit. A most striking illustration of this Old Testament mentality appears in relation to the downfall of King Saul. The biblical text indicates that "an evil spirit from the LORD tormented" Saul (1 Samuel 16:14; see also 16:15, 16, 23; 18:10; 19:9). It seems scandalous to consider that God was ever in the business of distributing evil spirits upon people. The earlier accounts of Saul's relationship with God made it clear, however, that Saul actually brought this upon himself through repeated acts of disobedience and self-reliance. Nevertheless, in the

Old Testament, "all things in the end are caused by the one God."[9] The point of these illustrations is to recognize that, though God took responsibility for the pain Israel endured, Israel was indeed liable for the wrongful actions that generated the consequences of its sins.

Often caught up with this Old Testament mentality is the attribution of anger to God (likely influenced by the view of gods in the ancient Near Eastern environment) when Israel suffered the consequences of sin. Such anger was sometimes expressed in the Old Testament to the point of depicting God as a tyrant who threw childlike tantrums (consider Exodus 32:7–14, which depicted Moses as a parent appearing to talk God down from an anger that sought to consume the people; see also Numbers 11:1–20). Hosea 11 worked against the grain of such depictions, declaring that God would not respond in fierce anger. While Israel's actions resulted in exile and dispersion, God acted to facilitate reconciliation. Any wrath of God was overwhelmed by the love of God. God's children, who found themselves in peril as a result of rejecting God in favor of the Baals, were called back to the loving arms of a gracious God whose authoritative roar provided safe passage home.

The final statement in Hosea 11 is one of restoration. God declared, "I will settle them in their houses" (v. 11b). A similar statement of restoration was proclaimed by the prophet Ezekiel:

> Thus says the Lord God, "When I gather the house of Israel from the peoples among whom they are scattered, and will manifest My holiness in them in the sight of the nations, then they will live in their land which I gave to my servant Jacob. They will live in it securely, and they will build houses, plant vineyards and live securely when I execute judgments upon all who scorn them round about them. Then they will know that I am the Lord their God." (Ezekiel 28:25–26, NASB).

9. Hans Wilhelm Hertzberg, *I & II Samuel, Old Testament Library* (Philadelphia: Westminster, 1976), 140–41.

The passage in Hosea 11 closes with a formulaic phrase, "oracle of the Lord" (see NABRE), which is commonly translated, "declares the Lord," or "says the Lord."[10] Hosea 11:12 then starts a new passage that begins another oracle. The Hebrew text makes this clear by ending Hosea 11 at verse 11, and numbering verse 12 as Hosea 12:1 (see also NABRE).

Conclusion

We are taught not to chastise our children from a state of anger. Doing so may cause one to act irrationally with out-of-control emotions, resulting in abuse and harm rather than reform. Though some Old Testament texts appear to depict God reacting in such ways in response to Israel's apostasy, Hosea 11 declares that God does not react with such human weakness (v. 9); rather, God responds with overwhelming love and compassion (v. 8). Clearly, this chapter in Hosea portrays God in humanlike ways (a parent, with heart and mind like a human, with human emotions of fierce anger and deep compassion). At the same time, however, verse 9 explicitly reminds the reader that God is not human. Meanwhile, the writers of the Old Testament *were* human and were often confined to human referents in their attempts to describe God and God's involvement in the world. This tendency was further influenced by an ancient Near Eastern environment that saw the gods as capricious and vindictive. Bible readers must sort through such dynamics as they seek to understand the overall message of the inspired text. In the case of Hosea 11, the message sought to emphasize the love and compassion of God for God's children.

Hosea 11 contributes to the groundwork laid by much of the Old Testament that finds fulfillment in the New Testament. The anguish God expressed over God's children, prompted by the tension be-

10. See Andersen and Freedman, *Hosea*, 592; and Hans Walter Wolff, *Hosea*, Hermeneia (Philadelphia: Fortress, 1974), 202–203.

tween wrath against the devastation of sin and an overwhelming love for humanity, was ultimately conveyed in the mystery of the cross. Instead of the death of a stubborn and rebellious son (Israel; see Deuteronomy 21:18–21)—a torment too great for God to bear (Hosea 11:8–9)—God endured the death of an obedient and righteous Son (Christ)! In Christ, God laid down God's own life on behalf of God's creatures. The mystery of the cross expresses the very message Hosea preached to Israel. God's love and compassion overwhelm wrath and restore God's people from sin and alienation. Hosea 11 revealed that God is a God of love through the metaphor of a caring parent who loved God's child from initial calling and nurturing (vv. 1–4), through the anguish of sin and rebellion (vv. 5–7), and ultimately with a passionate commitment to reconcile and restore (vv. 8–11).

Questions for Discussion

1. What was the purpose of judgment as expressed in the oracles of the Old Testament prophets? Do you think threats of judgment typically worked in relation to their purpose?
2. How does the metaphor of God as a parent as described in Hosea 11 impact your understanding of the character of God?
3. How does Hosea 11 change or reinforce your previous understanding of God's wrath and God's love?

Bibliography

Andersen, Francis I. and David Noel Freedman. *Hosea*. AB 24. New York: Doubleday, 1980.

Brown, Francis, S. R. Driver, and Charles A. Briggs. *A Hebrew and English Lexicon of the Old Testament*. Peabody, MA: Hendrickson, 1996.

Day, John. "Baal (Deity)." *Anchor Bible Dictionary,* vol. 1. Edited by David Noel Freedman. 6 vols. New York: Doubleday, 1992.

Dearman, J. Andrew. *The Book of Hosea*. NICOT. Grand Rapids: Eerdmans, 2010.

Hertzberg, Hans Wilhelm. *I & II Samuel*. OTL. Philadelphia: Westminster, 1976.

Mays, James Luther. *Hosea*. OTL. Philadelphia: Westminster, 1969.

Wolff, Hans Walter. *Anthropology of the Old Testament*. Translated by Margaret Kohl. Philadelphia: Fortress, 1974.

Wolff, Hans Walter. *Hosea*. Hermeneia. Philadelphia: Fortress, 1974.

ABOUT THE AUTHORS

Editors

Brad E. Kelle is professor of Old Testament and Hebrew at Point Loma Nazarene University. An ordained elder in the Church of the Nazarene, he is the author of numerous books and articles, including *Telling the Old Testament Story* and *Ezekiel* in the *New Beacon Bible Commentary* series.

Stephanie Smith Matthews is assistant professor of Old Testament and Hebrew at Point Loma Nazarene University. She is a licensed minister in the Church of the Nazarene and contributor in *Following Jesus: Prophet, Priest, King*, available from The Foundry Publishing.

Contributors

Timothy M. Green is dean of the Millard Reed School of Theology and Christian Ministry and professor of Old Testament Literature and Theology at Trevecca Nazarene University. An ordained elder in the Church of the Nazarene, he is the author of various publications including *The God Plot: Living with Holy Imagination* and *Hosea–Micah* in the *New Beacon Bible Commentary* series.

Mitchel Modine is professor of Old Testament at Asia-Pacific Nazarene Theological Seminary. He is an ordained elder in the Church of the Nazarene and the author of *Numbers: A Pastoral and Contextual Commentary.*

Marty Alan Michelson teaches Bible courses online for various universities, Nazarene Bible College, and Nazarene Theological Seminary. He has served churches in the U.S. and overseas and is licensed to practice as a professional counselor in Oregon.

Jennifer M. Matheny is assistant professor of Old Testament at Nazarene Theological Seminary. Her family has served for more than twenty years in ministry (in Kansas, Missouri, California, Oklahoma, Oregon, and Canada), and she is the author of *Joshua* in the *Illustrated Hebrew-English Old Testament* series.

Kevin J. Mellish is chair and professor of biblical studies at Olivet Nazarene University. In addition to several published articles and book chapters, he is the author of *1 and 2 Samuel* in the *New Beacon Bible Commentary* series.

Jim Edlin is emeritus professor of biblical literature and languages at Mid-America Nazarene University. He is the author of *Daniel*, *Ezra–Nehemiah*, and *Haggai–Malachi* in the *New Beacon Bible Commentary* series.

Stephen P. Riley is associate professor of Old Testament and Hebrew at Northwest Nazarene University. He is an ordained elder in the Church of the Nazarene and coeditor of *God Still Calls: Discerning God's Direction for Service.*

Michael G. VanZant is professor of biblical literature and Old Testament, and coordinator of online Christian ministry programs at Mount Vernon Nazarene University. He is an ordained elder in the Church of the Nazarene and contributor to the *New Interpreter's Dictionary of the Bible.*

Thomas J. King is professor of Old Testament at Nazarene Bible College. He is an ordained elder in the Church of the Nazarene and author of *Leviticus* in the *New Beacon Bible Commentary* series.